VOGUE KNITTING

CHUNKY KNITS

VOGUE KNITTING
CHUNKY KNITS

SOHO PUBLISHING COMPANY
NEW YORK

SOHO PUBLISHING COMPANY
233 Spring Street
New York, New York 10013

Library of Congress Cataloging-in-Publication Data

Vogue knitting chunky knits / [editor-in-chief, Trisha Malcolm]. -- 1st ed.
p. cm. – (Vogue knitting on the go!)
ISBN 1-931543-02-X
1. Knitting–Patterns. 2. Sweaters I. Title: Chunky knits. II. Malcolm,
Trisha, 1960- III. Series.

TT825 .V6473 2001
747.43'20432–dc21   00-066768

Manufactured in China

1 3 5 7 9 10 8 6 4 2

First Edition

TABLE OF CONTENTS

INTRODUCTION

What could be more satisfying than knitting a complete garment—even an adult-sized one—in just one weekend? How about turning out a smart accessory in one afternoon, finishing a gift before it's due, or simply completing that project you've started? Knitting with chunky yarns can make all these dreams—and more—come true. Like all designs featured in the Knitting on the Go series, the chunky-knit projects in this book make the most of busy schedules and precious spare time—and provide instant gratification, too.

The popularity of garments knit with thick, chunky yarns and large needles is a great boon to those who knit on the go—especially new knitters who are attempting their first full-sized projects. Dozens of luscious new yarns are now available to meet this demand, which also allows knitters to experiment with combining yarns to create sensational effects with color and texture.

But best of all is simply the speed with which chunky knits—such as the beautiful designs featured in this book—can be completed. You'll be amazed at what can be accomplished in the carpool, on a lunch break, or during the ten o'clock news. Try setting aside a few uninterrupted hours on a weekend or family vacation—when you find that's enough time to finish a hat or a sleeve, you'll be hooked. With chunky yarns, a few stitches can go a long, long way.

Got a moment to spare? Fill your knitting basket with chunky yarns, brandish your fattest needles, and get ready to **KNIT ON THE GO!**

THE BASICS

Knitting has never been more popular in modern times than it is right now, and the number of knitters picking up needles for the first time is fast-growing. This trend has happily coincided with a fashion focus on chunky knits: sweaters, tops, and accessories knit with thick, cushy yarns and large needles. With chunky knits, even beginners can experience the delight of finishing a large-scale project—such as a adult-sized sweater—in a relatively short period of time and with excellent results. Expert knitters, too, can enjoy watching a project, even one with challenging stitch patterns, work up in days, not months.

The projects in this book are designed with knitters of all skill levels in mind, and offer many creative opportunities for all. The Textured Turtleneck on page 55 ensures a satisfying accomplishment for a new knitter, while those with more experience will welcome the stitch patterns of the Child's Cabled Jacket on page 66. Knitters who love mixing colors will enjoy the possibilities posed by the Marled Turtleneck on page 77, and anyone searching for a quick summer fix will find just what they need among chic sleeveless tops.

SIZING

When determining what size sweater to make, measure a sweater that fits you well, then compare these measurements to those given in the "Knitted Measurements" section of the pattern.

GARMENT CONSTRUCTION

Aside from the traditional ways of knitting pieces and sewing them together, we have explored some more unusual techniques of sample making. The Cap-Sleeved Top on page 46 is worked in one piece from the top of the neck down to the lower edge. The sleeves on the Textured Turtleneck on page 55 are picked up at the armholes and decreased down to the cuff. Sewing with chunky yarns can make a thick seam; therefore, eliminating seams is always advisable. Even though most of the garments in this book are made in pieces, if you are a fairly experienced knitter, you can try knitting many of them in the round, or pick up your sleeve stitches at the underarm. You just need to make some simple adjustments to the pattern.

YARN SELECTION

For an exact reproduction of the projects photographed, use the yarn listed in the "Materials" section of the pattern. We've chosen yarns that are readily available in the U.S. and Canada at the time of printing. The Resources list on pages 94 and 95 provides addresses of yarn distributors. Contact them for the name of a retailer in your area.

YARN SUBSTITUTION

You may wish to substitute yarns. Perhaps you view small-scale projects as a chance to incorporate leftovers from your yarn stash, or the yarn specified may not be available in your area. You'll need to knit to the given gauge to obtain the knitted measurements with a substitute yarn (see "Gauge" on page 11). Be sure to consider how the fiber content of the substitute yarn will affect the comfort and the ease of care of your projects.

GAUGE

It is always important to knit a gauge swatch, and it is even more so with garments to ensure proper fit.

Patterns usually state gauge over a 4"/10cm span; however, it's beneficial to make a larger test swatch. This gives you a more precise stitch gauge, a better idea of the appearance and drape of the knitted fabric, and a chance to familiarize yourself with the stitch pattern.

The type of needles used—straight or circular, wood or metal—will influence gauge, so knit your swatch with the needles you plan to use for the project. Measure gauge as illustrated. Try different needle sizes until your sample measures the required number of stitches and rows. *To get fewer stitches to the inch/cm, use larger needles; to get more stitches to the inch/cm, use smaller needles.*

Knitting in the round may tighten the gauge, so if you measured the gauge on a flat swatch, take another gauge reading after you begin knitting. When the piece measures at least 2"/5cm, lay it flat and measure over the stitches in the center of the piece, as the side stitches may be distorted.

It's a good idea to keep your gauge swatch in order to test blocking and cleaning methods.

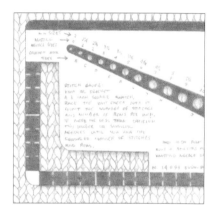

To facilitate yarn substitution, Vogue Knitting grades yarn by the standard stitch gauge obtained in stockinette stitch. You'll find a grading number in the "Materials" section of the pattern, immediately following the fiber type of the yarn. Look for a substitute yarn that falls into the same category. The suggested needle size and gauge on the yarn label should be comparable to that on the Yarn Symbols chart (see page 17).

After you've successfully gauge-swatched a substitute yarn, you'll need to figure out how much of the substitute yarn the project requires. First, find the total length of the original yarn in the pattern (multiply number of balls by yards/meters per ball). Divide this figure by the new yards/meters per ball (listed on the yarn label). Round up to the next whole number. The answer is the number of balls required.

FOLLOWING CHARTS

Charts are a convenient way to follow colorwork, lace, cable, and other stitch patterns at a glance. Vogue Knitting stitch charts utilize the universal knitting language of "symbolcraft." When knitting back and forth in rows, read charts from right to left on right side (RS) rows and from left to right on wrong side (WS) rows, repeating any stitch and row repeats as directed in the pattern. When knitting in the round, read charts from right to left on every round. Posting a self-adhesive note under your working row is an easy way to keep track of your place on a chart.

COLORWORK KNITTING

Two main types of colorwork are explored in this book.

Intarsia

Intarsia is accomplished with separate bobbins of individual colors. This method is ideal for large blocks of color or for motifs that aren't repeated close together. When changing colors, always pick up the new color and wrap it around the old color to prevent holes.

For smaller areas of color, such as the accent diamonds on the Woman's Argyle Vest (page 42), duplicate stitch embroidery is done after the pieces are knit.

Stranding

When motifs are closely placed, colorwork is accomplished by stranding along two or more colors per row, creating "floats" on the wrong side of the fabric. This technique is sometimes called Fair Isle knitting after the traditional Fair Isle patterns that are composed of small motifs with frequent color changes.

To keep an even tension and prevent holes while knitting, pick up yarns alternately over and under one another across or around. While knitting, stretch the stitches on the needle slightly wider than the length of the float at the back to keep work from puckering.

When changing colors at the beginning of rows or rounds, carry yarn along for a few rows only, or cut yarn and rejoin when needed. It is important to keep the floats small and neat so they don't catch when pulling on the piece.

BLOCKING

Blocking is an all-important finishing step in the knitting process. It is the best way to shape pattern pieces and smooth knitted edges in preparation for sewing together. Most garments retain their shape if the blocking stages in the instructions are followed carefully. Choose a blocking method according the the yarn care label and when in doubt, test-block your gauge swatch.

Wet Block Method

Using rust-proof pins, pin pieces to measurements on a flat surface and lightly dampen using a spray bottle. Allow to dry before removing pins.

Steam Block Method

With WS facing, pin pieces. Steam lightly, holding the iron 2"/5cm above the knitting. Do not press or it will flatten stitches.

FINISHING

The pieces in this book use a variety of finishing techniques from crocheting pieces together, as in the Striped Pillows on page 49, to joining shoulders with the three-needle bind-off method, used in the Woman's Vest on page 24. Directions for making pom-poms are on page 17, fringes are on page 14. Also refer to the illustrations provided for other useful techniques: knitting with double-pointed needles (shown on opposite page).

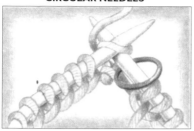

Hold the needle tip with the last cast-on stitch in your right hand and the tip with the first cast-on stitch in your left hand. Knit the first cast-on stitch, pulling the yarn tight to avoid a gap.

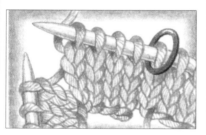

Work until you reach the marker. This completes the first round. Slip the marker to the right needle and work the next round.

SEWING

When using a very bulky or highly textured yarn, it is sometimes easier to seam pieces together with a finer, flat yarn. Just be sure that your sewing yarn closely matches the original yarn used in your project in color and washability.

CARE

Refer to the yarn label for the recommended cleaning method. Many of the projects

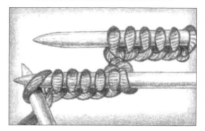

1 Cast on the required number of stitches on the first needle, plus one extra. Slip this extra stitch to the next needle as shown. Continue in this way, casting on the required number of stitches on the last needle.

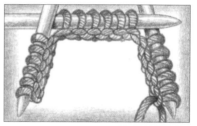

2 Arrange the needles as shown, with the cast-on edge facing the center of the triangle (or square).

3 Place a stitch marker after the last cast-on stitch. With the free needle, knit the first cast-on stitch, pulling the yarn tightly. Continue knitting in rounds, slipping the marker before beginning each round.

in the book can be either washed by hand or in the machine on a gentle or wool cycle, in lukewarm water with a mild detergent. Do not agitate or soak for more than 10 minutes. Rinse gently with tepid water, then fold in a towel and gently press the water out. Lay flat to dry away from excess heat and light. Check the yarn label for any specific care instructions such as dry cleaning or tumble drying.

FRINGE

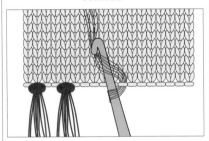

Simple fringe: Cut yarn twice desired length plus extra for knotting. On wrong side, insert hook from front to back through piece and over folded yarn. Pull yarn through. Draw ends through and tighten. Trim yarn.

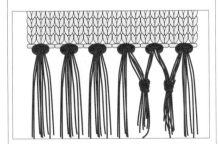

Knotted fringe: After working a simple fringe (it should be longer to allow for extra knotting), take one half of the strands from each fringe and knot them with half the strands from the neighboring fringe.

THREE-NEEDLE BIND-OFF

1 With RS placed together, hold pieces on two parallel needles. Insert a third needle knitwise into the first stitch of each needle, and wrap the yarn around the needle as if to knit.

2 Knit these two stitches together, and slip them off the needles. *Knit the next two stitches together in the same manner.

3 Slip the first stitch on the third needle over the second stitch and off the needle. Repeat from the * in Step 2 across the row until all stitches have been bound off.

TO BEGIN SEAMING

DUPLICATE STITCH

If you have left a long tail from your cast-on row, you can use this strand to begin sewing. To make a neat join at the lower edge with no gap, use the technique shown here. Thread the strand into a yarn needle. With the right sides of both pieces facing you, insert the yarn needle from back to front into the corner stitch of the piece without the tail. Making a figure eight with the yarn, insert the needle from back to front into the stitch with the cast-on tail. Tighten to close the gap.

INVISIBLE SEAMING: STOCKINETTE ST

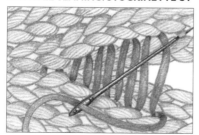

To make an invisible side seam in a garment worked in stockinette stitch, insert the yarn needle under the horizontal bar between the first and second stitches. Insert the needle into the corresponding bar on the other piece. Pull the yarn gently until the sides meet. Continue alternating from side to side.

Duplicate stitch covers a knit stitch. Bring the needle up below the stitch to be worked. Insert the needle under both loops one row above and pull it through. Insert it back into the stitch below and through the center of the next stitch in one motion, as shown.

CROCHET STITCHES

CHAIN

1 *Pass the yarn over the hook and catch it with the hook.*

2 *Draw the yarn through the loop on the hook.*

3 *Repeat steps 1 and 2 to make a chain.*

SINGLE CROCHET

1 *Insert the hook through top two loops of a stitch. Pass the yarn over the hook and draw up a loop—two loops on hook.*

2 *Pass the yarn over the hook and draw through both loops on hook.*

3 *Continue in the same way, inserting the hook into each stitch.*

HALF-DOUBLE CROCHET

1 *Pass the yarn over the hook. Insert the hook through the top two loops of a stitch.*

2 *Pass the yarn over the hook and draw up a loop—three loops on hook. Pass the yarn over the hook.*

3 *Draw through all three loops on hook.*

DOUBLE CROCHET

1 *Pass the yarn over the hook. Insert the hook through the top two loops of a stitch.*

2 *Pass the yarn over the hook and draw up a loop— three loops on hook.*

3 *Pass the yarn over the hook and draw it through the first two loops on the hook, pass the yarn over the hook and draw through the remaining two loops. Continue in the same way, inserting the hook into each stitch.*

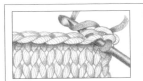

SLIP STITCH

Insert the crochet hook into a stitch, catch the yarn and pull up a loop. Draw the loop through the loop on the hook.

Illustrations: Joni Coniglio

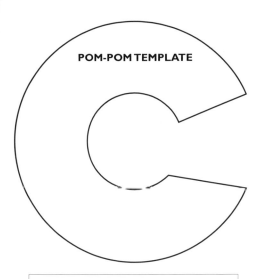

POM-POM TEMPLATE

① **Fine Weight**
(29-32 stitches per 4"/10cm)
Includes baby and fingering yarns, and some of the heavier crochet cottons. The range of needle sizes is 0-4 (2-3.5mm).

② **Lightweight**
(25-28 stitches per 4"/10cm)
Includes sport yarn, sock yarn, UK 4-ply, and lightweight DK yarns. The range of needle sizes is 3-6 (3.25-4mm).

③ **Medium Weight**
(21-24 stitches per 4"/10cm)
Includes DK and worsted, the most commonly used knitting yarns. The range of needle sizes is 6-9 (4-5.5mm).

POM-POMS

1 Following the template, cut two circular pieces of cardboard.

2 Hold the two circles together and wrap the yarn tightly around the cardboard several times. Secure and carefully cut the yarn.

④ **Medium-heavy Weight**
(17-20 stitches per 4"/10cm)
Also called heavy worsted or Aran. The range of needle sizes is 8-10 (5-6mm).

⑤ **Bulky Weight**
(13-16 stitches per 4"/10cm)
Also called chunky. Includes heavier Icelandic yarns. The range of needle sizes is 10-11 (6-8mm).

3 Tie a piece of yarn tightly between the two circles. Remove the cardboard and trim the pom-pom to the desired size.

⑥ **Extra-bulky Weight**
(9-12 stitches per 4"/10cm)
The heaviest yarns available. The range of needle sizes is 11 and up (8mm and up).

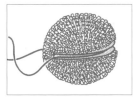

KNITTING TERMS AND ABBREVIATIONS

approx approximately

beg begin(ning)

bind off Used to finish an edge and keep stitches from unraveling. Lift the first stitch over the second, the second over the third, etc. (UK: cast off)

cast on A foundation row of stitches placed on the needle in order to begin knitting.

CC contrast color

ch chain(s)

cm centimeter(s)

cont continue(ing)

dc double crochet (UK: tr-treble)

dec decrease(ing)–Reduce the stitches in a row (knit 2 together).

dpn double-pointed needle(s)

foll follow(s)(ing)

g gram(s)

garter stitch Knit every row. Circular knitting: knit one round, then purl one round.

hdc half double crochet (UK: htr-half treble)

inc increase(ing)–Add stitches in a row (knit into the front and back of a stitch).

k knit

k2tog knit 2 stitches together

LH left-hand

lp(s) loop(s)

m meter(s)

M1 make one stitch–With the needle tip, lift the strand between last stitch worked and next stitch on the left-hand needle and knit into the back of it. One knit stitch has been added.

M1-p make one purl stitch–With the needle tip, lift the strand between last stitch worked and next stitch on the left-hand needle and purl into the back of it. One purl stitch has been added.

MC main color

mm millimeter(s)

no stitch On some charts, "no stitch" is indicated with shaded spaces where stitches have been decreased or not yet made. In such cases, work the stitches of the chart, skipping over the "no stitch" spaces.

oz ounce(s)

p purl

p2tog purl 2 stitches together

pat(s) pattern

pick up and knit (purl) Knit (or purl) into the loops along an edge.

pm place markers–Place or attach a loop of contrast yarn or purchased stitch marker as indicated.

psso pass slip stitch(es) over

rem remain(s)(ing)

rep repeat

rev St st reverse Stockinette stitch–Purl right-side rows, knit wrong-side rows. Circular knitting: purl all rounds. (UK: reverse stocking stitch)

rnd(s) round(s)

RH right-hand

RS right side(s)

sc single crochet (UK: dc-double crochet)

sk skip

SKP Slip 1, knit 1, pass slip stitch over knit 1.

SK2P Slip 1, knit 2 together, pass slip stitch over the knit 2 together.

sl slip–An unworked stitch made by passing a stitch from the left-hand to the right-hand needle as if to purl.

sl st slip stitch (UK: single crochet)

ssk slip, slip, knit–Slip next 2 stitches knitwise, one at a time, to right-hand needle. Insert tip of left-hand needle into fronts of these stitches from left to right. Knit them

together. One stitch has been decreased.

sssk Slip next 3 sts knitwise, one at a time, to right-hand needle. Insert tip of left-hand needle into fronts of these stitches from left to right. Knit them together. Two stitches have been decreased.

st(s) stitch(es)

St st Stockinette stitch–Knit right-side rows, purl wrong-side rows. Circular knitting: knit all rounds. (UK: stocking stitch)

tbl through back of loop

tog together

WS wrong side(s)

wyib with yarn in back

wyif with yarn in front

work even Continue in pattern without increasing or decreasing. (UK: work straight)

yd yard(s)

yo yarn over–Make a new stitch by wrapping the yarn over the right-hand needle. (UK: yfwd, yon, yrn)

* = repeat directions following * as many times as indicated.

[ ] = Repeat directions inside brackets as many times as indicated.

COLORBLOCKED TURTLENECK

Need for tweed

Bold blocks of color are angled to follow the A-line shape of Mari Lynn Patrick's tweedy turtleneck. Raglan sleeves accentuate the streamlined look, and rolled edges provide contrasting trim.

SIZES
Instructions are written for size Small. Changes for sizes Medium and Large are in parentheses.

KNITTED MEASUREMENTS
- Lower edge 44 (47, 49)"/111.5 (119, 124.5)cm
- Bust 39 (41, 44)"/99 (104, 111.5)cm
- Length 27 (28, 29)"/68.5 (71, 73.5)cm
- Upper arm 15 (16½, 17½)"/38 (42, 44.5)cm

MATERIALS
- 2 3½oz/100g hanks (each approx 109yd/100m) of Rowan Yarns *Chunky Tweed* (wool⑥) each in #880 black (A), #953 olive (B) and #950 brown (C)
- 1 hank each in #952 lt blue (D), #887 plum (F) and #888 navy (G)
- 1 (1, 2) hanks in #954 orange (E)
- One pair each sizes 10 and 10½ (6 and 6.5mm) needles *or size to obtain gauge*

GAUGE
12 sts and 17 rows to 4"/10cm over St st using larger needles.
Take time to check gauge.

Note
Chart for front and back is drawn without selvage sts. Therefore, st counts in instructions reflect 2 extra sts not shown on chart.

BACK
With smaller needles and A, cast on 68 (72, 76) sts. K 1 row, p 1 row. Change to larger needles.

Beg chart pat
Row 1 (WS) With F, k1 (selvage st), p16 (18, 20), with B, p34, with D, p16 (18, 20), k1 (selvage st). Cont to work in this way foll chart, dec 1 st each side every 18th row 4 times—60 (64, 68) sts. Work even for 6 rows more.

Raglan armhole shaping
Bind off 2 sts at beg of next 2 rows.
Dec row (RS) K4, k3tog, k to last 7 sts, SK2P, k4. Work 3 rows even. Rep last 4 rows 4 (5, 6) times more. Work dec row on next row, then every other row 3 times more. Work 1 row even, then bind off rem 20 sts.

FRONT
Work as for back foll chart to neck shaping.
Next row (RS) Bind off center 4 sts. Working both sides at once, work 1 row even, then dec 1 st at each neck edge on next row. Work 1 row even. Bind off rem 7 sts each side to shape neck.

LEFT SLEEVE
Work in stripe pat for 33 rows D, 30 rows E, 26 rows G and rem of sleeve with C.

With smaller needles and A, cast on 27 (29, 31) sts. K 1 row, p 1 row. Change to larger needles and D. Cont in St st and stripe pat, inc 1 st each side (inside of selvage sts) every 6th row 10 (11, 12) times—47 (51, 55) sts. Work even until there are same number of rows (16 rows) in 3rd color stripe in G as on back.

Raglan cap shaping

Bind off 2 sts at beg of next 2 rows.

Dec row (RS) K3, k3tog, k to last 6 sts, SK2P, k3. Rep dec row every 4th row 7 (8, 9) times more—11 sts. Work even for 1 row (or until sleeve fits back or front armhole). Bind off.

RIGHT SLEEVE

Work as for left sleeve foll this color sequence: 33 rows F, 30 rows C, 26 rows B and rem of sleeve with E.

FINISHING

Block pieces to measurements. Sew sleeves into armholes leaving one seam open.

Collar

With smaller needles and A, pick up and k 63 sts evenly around neck edge. Work in k1, p1 rib for 1¾"/4.5cm. Change to larger needles and work in rib for 1¾"/4.5cm more. Bind off in rib. Sew other raglan seam and collar. Sew side and sleeve seams.

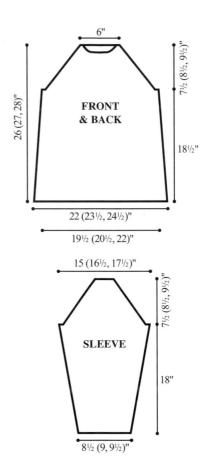

FRONT & BACK

6"

7½ (8½, 9½)"

26 (27, 28)"

18½"

22 (23½, 24½)"

19½ (20½, 22)"

15 (16½, 17½)"

SLEEVE

7½ (8½, 9½)"

18"

8½ (9, 9½)"

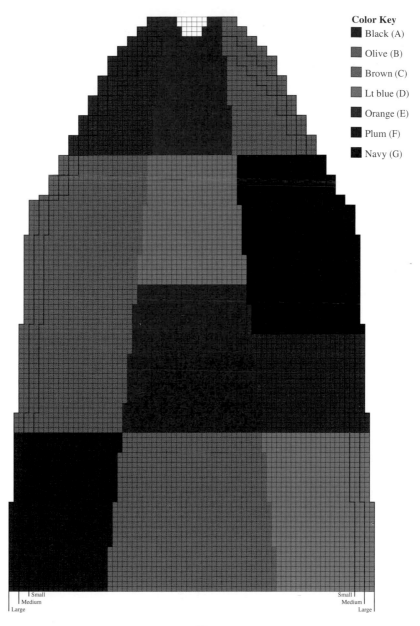

WOMAN'S VEST

Cable vision

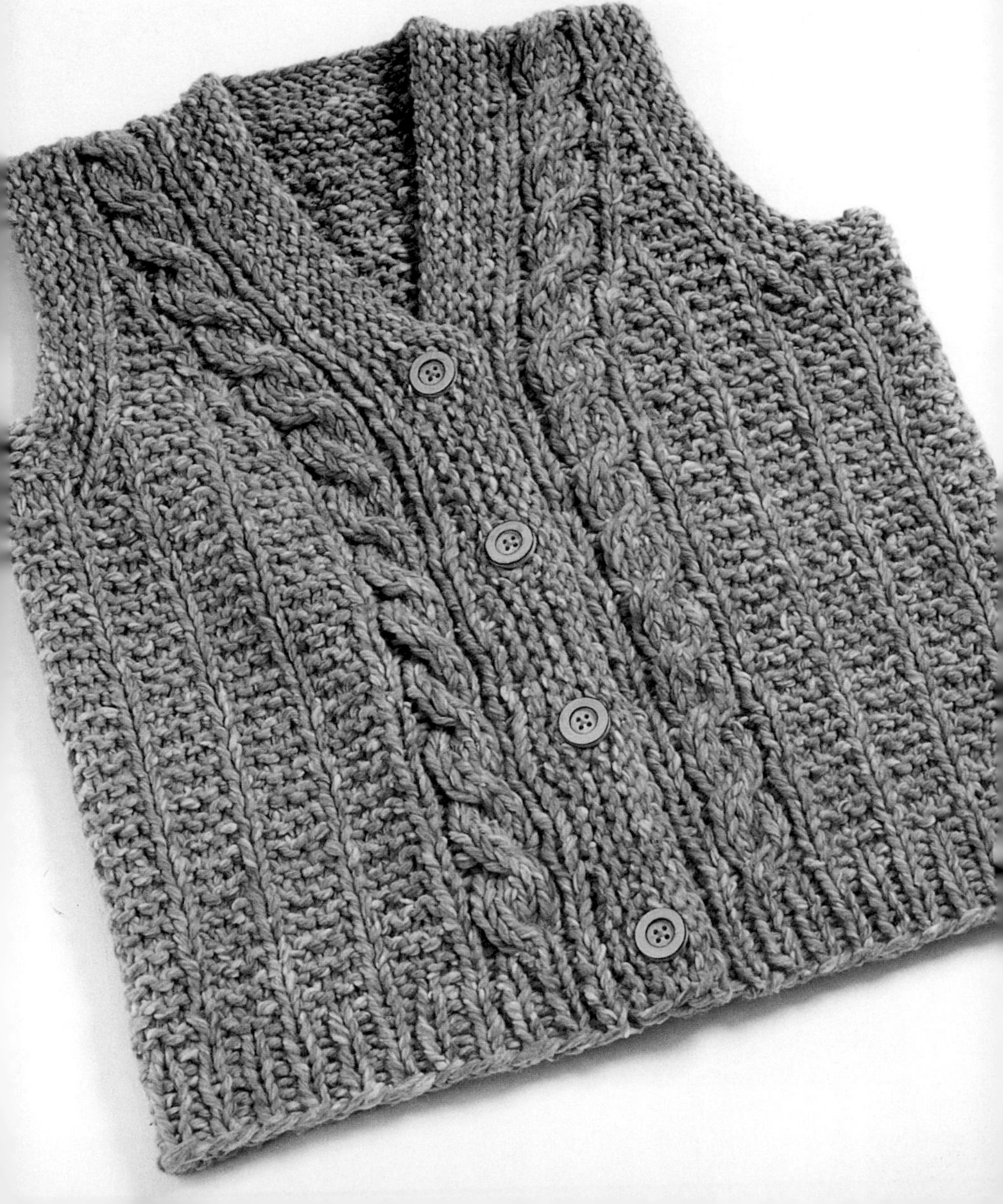

For Intermediate Knitters

Pattern stitches abound in E. J. Slayton's ladder-stitch vest. A single cable encircles the front and V-neck edges, and garter-stitch borders finish off the armholes and button bands.

KNITTED MEASUREMENTS
- Bust (buttoned) 35 (38, 41, 46)"/89 (96.5, 104, 117)cm
- Length 19½ (20, 21½, 21½)"/49.5 (50.5, 54.5, 54.5)cm

MATERIALS
- 6 (7, 7, 8) 1¾ oz/50g balls (each approx 55yd/50m) of Lane Borgosesia *Levante* (wool/nylon ⑤) in #164 blue
- One pair each sizes 10 and 10½ (6mm and 7mm) needles *or size to obtain gauge*
- Size 10 (6mm) circular needle, 24"/60cm or 29"/74cm long
- Cable needle
- Stitch markers
- Stitch holders
- Tapestry needle
- Five ¾"/20mm buttons

GAUGE
11 sts and 18 rows to 4"/10cm over ladder st using larger needles.
Take time to check gauge.

LADDER STITCH
Row 1 (RS) Knit.
Row 2 P1, *k3, p1; rep from * to end.
Rep rows 1 and 2 for ladder st.

BACK
With smaller needles, cast on 47 (51, 55, 63) sts. Work in k1, p1 rib as foll:
Row 1 (WS) P2, *k1, p1; rep from * to last 3 sts, end k1, p2.
Row 2 K2, *p1, k1; rep from * to last 3 sts, end p1, k2.
Rep rows 1 and 2 until piece measures 2"/5cm from beg, end with a WS row. Change to larger needles.

BEG LADDER ST
Row 1 (RS) Knit.
Row 2 P2, k3 (3, 1, 3), *p1, k3; rep from * to last 6 sts, p1, k3 (3, 1, 3), p2.
Rep last 2 rows until piece measures 12 (12, 13, 13)"/30.5 (30.5, 33, 33)cm from beg.
Armhole shaping
Bind off 5 (5, 6, 8) sts at beg of next 2 rows. Dec 1 st each side on next row, then every other row twice more—31 (35, 37, 41) sts. Cont in pat until armhole measures 7½ (8, 8½, 8½)"/19 (20, 21.5, 21.5)cm, end with a WS row. Place first 6 (7, 8, 9) sts on a holder for right shoulder, place center 19 (21, 21, 23) sts on a second holder for back neck, place rem 6 (7, 8, 9) sts on a third holder for left shoulder.

RIGHT FRONT
With smaller needles, cast on 25 (27, 29,

32) sts. Work in k1, p1 rib as for back, end with a WS row. Change to larger needles.

BEG LADDER ST AND CABLE PAT

Row 1 (RS) K2, pm, p1, k1, k in front and back of next st, k1, p1, pm, k to end—26 (28, 30, 33) sts.

Rows 2, 4 and 6 P2, k3 (3, 1, 3), p1, *k3, p1, rep from * to first marker, end k1, p4, k1, p2.

Row 3 K2, p1, sl next 2 sts to cn and hold in *front*, k2, k2 from cn, p1, k to end.

Rows 5 and 7 K2, p1, k4, p1, k to end.

Rep rows 2–7 for pat until piece measures 12 (12, 13, 13)"/30.5 (30.5, 33, 33)cm from beg, end with a RS row.

Armhole and neck shaping

Next row (WS) Bind off 5 (5, 6, 8) sts, work to end. Work 1 row even. Dec 1 st at beg of next row, then every other row twice more, AT SAME TIME, work neck dec on RS rows as foll: Work pat across first 8 sts, ssk, work to end. Rep neck dec every other row 1 (0, 0, 0) time more, then alternately [every 4th row and every other row] until there are 10 (11, 12, 13) sts. Work even in pat until piece measures same as back to shoulder, end with a WS row.

Shoulder shaping

Next row (RS) K1, ssk twice, k2tog twice, k1 (2, 3, 4)—6 (7, 8, 9) sts. Bind off front and back shoulder sts tog using 3-needle bind-off.

LEFT FRONT

Work to correspond to right front, revers-ing pat placement and shaping, and work-ing 4-st cable as foll: sl next 2 sts to cn and hold in *back*, k2, k2 from cn.

FINISHING

Block pieces to measurments.

Armhole bands

With RS facing and smaller needles, beg at underarm, pick up and k sts as foll: 1 st in each bound-off st of underarm, pm, 2 sts for every 3 rows around armhole edge, pm, and 1 st in each bound-off st at other side of underarm.

Row 1 (WS) Sl 1, k to end.

Row 2 *K to 2 sts before marker, k2tog, k1, ssk; rep from * once more, k to end.

Rows 3–5 Rep rows 1 and 2, ending with Row 1.

Bind off all sts purlwise on RS.

Sew side seams.

FRONT BAND

With RS facing and smaller needles, beg at lower edge of right front, pick up and k 2 sts for every 3 rows to beg of neck shaping, pm, 3 sts for every 4 rows to shoulder, k across back neck sts, pick up and k sts along left front to match right front, placing marker at neck.

Row 1 Sl 1, k to end.

Row 2 Sl 1, k to marker, sl marker, M1, k to second marker, M1, sl marker, k to end.

Row 3 Rep row 1. Mark right front for 5 even-ly spaced buttonholes, beg 3 sts from lower edge and ending at beg of neck shaping.

Row 4 Work as row 2, working buttonholes as foll: Work to buttonhole marker, sl next st, bring yarn to front and drop it. *Sl next st, pass first st over it; rep from * once more (2 sts bound-off), then replace st on LH needle in a twisted position. Take yarn over tip of RH needle, pass last st on needle over it, cast on 3 sts with tight backward loops, k next 2 sts tog. On next row, k in back of st each loop and st on each side of buttonhole.

Row 5 Sl 1, k across, completing buttonholes.
Row 6 Rep row 2.
Row 7 Rep row 1.

Bind off all sts purlwise on RS. Sew buttons on left band opposite buttonholes.

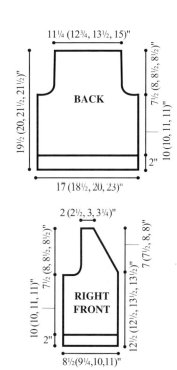

11¼ (12¾, 13½, 15)"

7½ (8, 8½, 8½)"

BACK

10 (10, 11, 11)"

19½ (20, 21½, 21½)"

2"

17 (18½, 20, 23)"

2 (2½, 3, 3¼)"

7½ (8, 8½, 8½)"

7 (7½, 8, 8)"

10 (10, 11, 11)"

RIGHT FRONT

12½ (12½, 13¼, 13½)"

2"

8½ (9¼, 10, 11)"

KILIM TOTE
Carpetbag

Jewel tones and a thick, fleecy yarn add exotic appeal to this sophisticated handbag, designed by Lipp Holmfeld. Rattan handles top it off, while a sewn-in lining gives valuables a smooth ride.

KNITTED MEASUREMENTS

- 11½"/29cm wide x 12"/30.5cm tall

MATERIALS

- 2 1¾oz/50g balls (each approx 48yds/44m) of K1C2, LLC *Flureece* (wool/nylon⑤) in #900 black (A)
- 1 ball each in #212 burgundy (B), #835 orange (C), #565 green (D) and #713 purple (E)
- One pair size 8 (5mm) needles *or size to obtain gauge*
- Tapestry needle
- 1 piece of cotton fabric, 26" x 11½"/66cm x 29cm
- 1 piece of cardboard, 9½" x 3"/24cm x 7.5cm with rounded corners
- 2 rattan handles, large vintage, D shape

GAUGE

10 sts and 12 rows to 4"/10cm over St st and chart pat using size 8 (5mm) needles. *Take time to check gauge.*

BAG

With A, cast on 18 sts. Beg with a RS row, work in St st for 6 rows, cast on 5 sts at end of last WS row. **Next row (RS)** K 23, cast on 5 sts—28 sts. Work even for 3 rows. **Beg chart (first side)**
Next row (RS) Cont in St st, beg with row 1 (at top of chart) and work rows 1-32. **Next row (RS)** Change to A and cont in St st for 12 rows.
Beg chart (second side)
Next row (RS) Cont in St st, beg with row 32 (at bottom of chart) and work rows 32-1. **Next row (RS)** Change to A and cont in St st for 3 rows. **Next row (RS)** Bind off 5 sts at beg of next 2 rows. Bind off rem 18 sts.

FINISHING

With A, sew sides of bag together. Sew across corners on bottom, tucking corners in. Place cardboard under tucks at the bottom. On both sides of bag, bend narrow pieces on top around handles. Stitch down. Fold lining in half, stitch closed on sides with ½"/1cm seam allowance. Sew across corners as for outside of bag. Place inside bag and fold on top to fit. Stitch around top of bag.

Color Key
- ■ Black (A)
- ■ Burgundy (B)
- ■ Orange (C)
- ■ Green (D)
- ■ Purple (E)

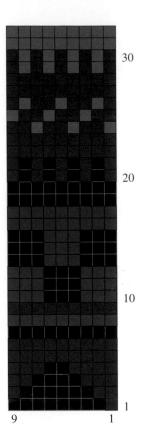

Short and stylish, Kellie Overbey's cropped cardigan can be worn buttoned down the front or back. The raglan sleeves, seed-stitch edgings, and self-finishing make it even more clever. Short-row shaping for the neck adds a touch of tailoring.

SIZES

Instructions are written for size X-Small/Small. Changes for sizes Medium and Large are in parentheses.

KNITTED MEASUREMENTS

- Bust (buttoned) 32 (36, 40)"/81.5 (91.5, 101.5)cm
- Length 19 (19½, 20)"/48.5 (49.5, 51)cm
- Upper arm 13 (15, 16¼)"/33 (38, 41.5)cm

MATERIALS

- 7 (9, 9) 3½oz/100g balls (each approx 88yd/80m) of Karabella *Softig* (cotton⑥) in #102 coral
- One pair size 13 (9mm) needles *or size to obtain gauge*
- Five ¾"/20mm buttons

GAUGE

12 sts and 16 rows to 4"/10cm over St st using size 13 (9mm) needles.
Take time to check gauge.

SEED STITCH

Row 1 (RS) *K1, p1; rep from * to end.

Row 2 K the purl sts and p the knit sts.
Rep rows 1 and 2 for seed st.

FRONT

Cast on 48 (54, 60) sts and work in seed st for 3 rows. **Next row (WS)** Purl. Work in St st until piece measures 10½"/26.5cm from beg, end with a WS row.

Raglan armhole shaping

Bind off 2 (3, 4) sts at beg of next 2 rows, 2 (3, 3) sts at beg of next 2 rows—40 (42, 46) sts. Work 0 (2, 0) rows even.
Next (dec) row (RS) K2, SKP, work to last 4 sts, k2tog, k2. Cont to work dec row every 4th row 4 (4, 5) times more—30 (32, 34) sts. Work 1 more row even, then beg neck shaping.

Neck shaping

Note

Each shoulder is worked separately in short rows. At the end of each short row, before turning the work, you must wrap a stitch as foll: If your last st is a knit st, bring yarn to the front, sl 1 st purlwise, bring yarn to back, return sl st to LH needle. If your last st is a purl st, bring yarn to the back, sl 1 st purlwise, bring yarn to the front and return sl st to LH needle.

Left shoulder

Next row (RS) K12, wrap a st, turn work. **Next and all WS rows** Purl. **Next row (RS)** K2, SKP, k6, wrap a st, turn work. **Next row (RS)** K7, wrap a st, turn work. **Next row (RS)** K2, SKP, k1, wrap a st, turn work. **Next row (RS)** K2, wrap a st, turn work. **Next row (WS)** Purl. Cut yarn. Sl all 28 (30, 32) sts to RH needle. Join yarn and beg right shoulder.

Right shoulder

Next row (WS) P12, wrap a st, turn work. **Next and all RS rows** Knit. **Next row (WS)** P2, p2tog, p6, wrap a st, turn work. **Next row (WS)** P7, wrap a st, turn work. **Next row (WS)** P2, p2tog, p1, wrap a st, turn work. **Next row (WS)** P2, wrap a st, turn work. **Next row (RS)** Knit. **Next row (WS)** Purl across all 26 (28, 30) sts, hiding wraps across row. Purl to a wrapped st, then hide as foll: **Right shoulder wrapped sts (first 5 wraps)** Pass the wrapped st from LH needle to RH needle purlwise. Unwrap the st by lifting the wrap onto the RH needle over the st just passed. Pass both sts back to the LH needle and purl them tog tbl. **Left shoulder wrapped sts (last 5 wraps)** Unwrap st by passing the wrap over it, keeping both sts on the LH needle. Purl them tog. **Next row (RS)** Bind off all sts.

RIGHT BACK

Cast on 27 (30, 33) sts and work in seed st for 3 rows. **Next row (WS)** Purl. **Next row and all RS rows** Knit across, slipping the last st of the row knitwise. Cont in St st until piece measures same length as back to raglan armhole shaping, end with a WS row.

Raglan armhole shaping

Next row (RS) Cont to sl last st of RS rows, bind off 2 (3, 4) sts at beg of row (armhole edge), then 2 (3, 3) sts at beg of next RS row—23 (24, 26) sts. Work 1 (3, 1) more rows even. **Next (dec) row (RS)** K2, SKP, k to last st, sl 1 knitwise. Cont to work dec row every 4th row (5, 5, 6) times more, AT SAME TIME, after first dec row has been worked, work 3 rows even, then beg neck shaping.

Neck shaping

Next row (RS) K2, SKP, k to last 4 sts, k2tog, k1, sl 1 knitwise. Work 1 row even. **Next row (RS)** K to last 4 sts, k2tog, k1, sl 1 knitwise. Cont as established, working raglan armhole shaping at armhole edge, slipping the last st on RS rows, and dec 1 st every other row at neck edge until 7 (8, 7) sts rem. Work 1 row even. **Next row (RS)** K2, k3tog, k1 (2, 1), sl 1 knitwise—5 (6, 5) sts. Work 1 row even. **Next row (RS)** K1, k3tog, k0 (1, 0), sl 1 knitwise—3 (4, 3) sts. Work 1 row even. Bind off all sts.

LEFT BACK

Cast on 27 (30, 33) sts and work in seed st for 3 rows. **Next row (WS)** Purl. **Next row and all RS rows** Slip the first st of the row knitwise, knit to end. Cont in St st until piece measures same length as right back to raglan armhole shaping, end with a RS row, AT SAME TIME, work buttonholes as foll: When piece measures 2 (2½, 2)"/5 (6.5, 5)cm from beg, end with a WS row. **Next (buttonhole) row (RS)** Sl 1 knitwise, k1, SKP, work to end. **Next row (WS)** P to last 2 sts, end yo, p2. Cont to work buttonhole row every 10th row 4 times more.

Raglan armhole shaping

Next row (WS) Cont to sl first st of RS rows, bind off 2 (3, 4) sts at beg of row (armhole edge), then 2 (3, 3) sts at beg of next WS row—23 (24, 26) sts. Work 0 (2, 0) rows even. **Next (dec) row (RS)** Sl 1 knitwise, k to last 4 sts, k2tog, k2. Cont to work dec row every 4th row (5, 5, 6) times more, AT SAME TIME, after first dec row has been worked, work 3 rows even then beg neck shaping.

Neck shaping

Next row (RS) Sl 1 knitwise, k1, SKP, k to last 4 sts, k2tog, k2. Work 1 row even. **Next row (RS)** Sl 1 knitwise, k1, SKP, k to end. Cont as established, working raglan armhole shaping at armhole edge, slipping the first st on RS rows and dec 1 every other row at neck edge until 7 (8, 7) sts rem. Work 1 row even. **Next row (RS)** Sl 1 knitwise, k1 (2, 1), [sl 2, k1, p2sso], k2—5 (6, 5) sts. Work 1 row even. **Next row (RS)** Sl 1 knitwise, k0 (1, 0), [sl 2, k1, p2sso], k1—3 (4, 3) sts. Work 1 row even. Bind off all sts.

SLEEVES

Cast on 35 (37, 41) sts and work in seed st for 3 rows. **Next row (WS)** Purl. Work in St st until piece measures 5½ (3, 3)"/14 (7.5, 7.5)cm from beg, end with a WS row. **Next (inc) row (RS)** K2, M1, work to last 2 sts, M1, k2—37 (39, 43) sts. Rep inc row every 4½ (2¾, 2¾)"/11.5 (7, 7)cm 1 (3, 3) times more—39 (45, 49) sts. Work even until piece measures 14"/35.5cm, from beg, end with a WS row.

Raglan cap shaping

Bind off 2 (3, 4) sts at beg of next 2 rows, 2 (3, 3) sts at beg of next 2 rows—31 (33, 35) sts. Work 0 (2, 0) rows even. **Next (dec) row (RS)** K2, SKP, work to last 4 sts, k2tog, k2. Work 3 (1, 3) rows even. Work dec row on next and every foll RS row 11 (12, 13) times more—7 sts. Work 1 more row even.

Note Right sleeve and left sleeve are worked differently to end. Work last 4 rows of right sleeve as foll: **Next row (RS)** K2, [sl 2, k1, p2sso], k2—5 sts. Work 1 row even. **Next row (RS)** K1, [sl 2, k1, p2sso], k1—3 sts. Work 1 row even. Bind off rem sts. Work last 4 rows of left sleeve as foll: **Next row (RS)** K2, k3tog, k2—5 sts. Work 1 row even. **Next row (RS)** K1, k3tog, k1—3 sts. Work 1 row even. Bind off rem sts.

FINISHING

Block pieces to measurement. Sew front to back pieces. Sew raglan sleeve caps into raglan armholes. Sew side and sleeve seams. Sew buttons on right back opposite buttonholes.

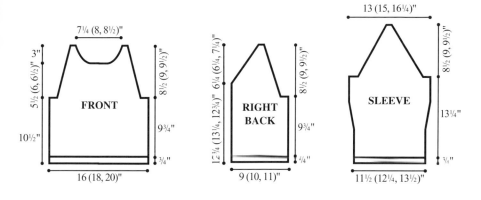

FRONT

7¼ (8, 8½)"

3"

5½ (6, 6½)"

8½ (9, 9½)"

9¾"

10½"

¾"

16 (18, 20)"

**RIGHT
BACK**

6¼ (6¼, 7¼)"

12¾ (13¼, 12¾)"

8½ (9, 9½)"

9¾"

¼"

9 (10, 11)"

SLEEVE

13 (15, 16¼)"

8½ (9, 9½)"

13¼"

¾"

11½ (12¼, 13½)"

STRIPED PULLOVER
Lace it up!

Irina Poludnenko's striped tunic showcases unique details. Diagonal stripes on the sides are formed by full-fashioning decreases, garter-stitch plackets are laced at the neck and wrists, and a garter-stitch border follows the shaped lower edge.

SIZES

Instructions are written for size Small. Changes for sizes Medium and Large are in parentheses.

KNITTED MEASUREMENTS

- Bust 40 (43, 46)"/101.5 (109, 116.5)cm
- Length 26½ (27, 27½)"/67 (68.5, 69.5)cm
- Upper arm 19 (20, 21)"/48 (50.5, 53)cm

MATERIALS

- 10 (11, 12) 2½oz/75g balls (each approx 49yd/45m) of Berroco, Inc *O2* (wool/acrylic⑤) in #9501 ivory (A)
- 8 (9, 10) balls in # 9539 green (B)
- One pair size 15 (10mm) needles *or size to obtain gauge*
- Size K/10.5 (6.5mm) crochet hook
- Stitch holders

GAUGE

10 sts and 14 rows to 4"/10cm over St st using size 15 (10mm) needles.
Take time to check gauge.

STRIPE PATTERN

*Work 4 rows A, 4 rows B; rep from * (8 rows) for stripe pat.

BACK

With A, cast on 50 (54, 58) sts. Knit 4 rows. Beg with B, cont in St st and stripe pat as foll:

Next row (RS) K1, M1, k9, k2tog, k26 (30, 34), ssk, k9, M1, k1.

Next row Purl. Rep last 2 rows until piece measures 16"/40.5cm from beg, end with a WS row.

Armhole shaping

Next row (RS) K10, k2tog, pm, k26 (30, 34), pm, ssk, k10. P 1 row.

Next row K to 2 sts before first marker, k2tog, sl marker, work to 2nd marker, sl marker, ssk, k to end. P 1 row. Rep last 2 rows 7 (8, 10) times more—32 (34, 34) sts. Work even until armhole measures 9½ (10, 10½)"/24 (25.5, 26.5)cm.

Shoulder shaping

Bind off 4 sts at beg of next 2 rows, 3 (4, 4) sts at beg of next 2 rows. Place rem 18 sts on holder for neck.

FRONT

Work as for back until piece measures 21 (21½, 22)"/53 (54.5, 56)cm from beg, end with a WS row.

Placket shaping

Next row (RS) Work 10 (11, 11) sts, place center 12 sts on a holder, join 2nd ball of yarn and work to end. Working both sides at once, work 16 rows even.

Neck and shoulder shaping

Dec 1 st at each neck edge on next row, then *every* row twice more, AT SAME TIME, when same length as back to shoulder, shape shoulders as for back.

SLEEVES

First part

With larger needles and A, cast on 12 sts. K 2 rows. **Next row (RS)** K9, yo, k2tog, k1. **Next row** Knit. Change to B, k7, leave rem 5 sts on holder. Cont in stripe pat for 12 rows more, AT SAME TIME, inc 1 st at beg of every 4th row twice—9 sts. Place these sts on second holder. Place 5 sts from first holder on needle and k 4 rows. **Eyelet row (RS)** K2, yo, k2tog, k1. K 5 rows. **Next row** Rep eyelet row. K 3 rows. Leave 5 sts on holder.

Second part

Work as for first part, reversing all shaping.

Joining row

From first part, k1, M1, k8 from first holder, from second holder k5, from second part k8, M1, k1 from first holder, from second holder k5—30 sts. **Next row (WS)** P10, k10, p10. **Next row** K12, yo, k2tog, k3, yo, k2tog, k11. **Next row** P10, k10, p10. Cont in St st and stripe pat, inc 1 st each side every 4th row 9 (10, 11) times—48 (50, 52) sts. Work even until piece measures 17"/43cm from beg.

Cap shaping

Work same as back armohle shaping. Bind off rem 30 (30, 28) sts.

FINISHING

Sew shoulder seams. Set in sleeves. sew side and sleeve seams.

Front neck bands

Pick up 12 sts from holder, k 2 rows. **Next row (RS)** K2, yo, k2tog, k3, yo, k2tog, k1. **Next row** Knit. **Next row** K6, place rem 6 sts on holder. K 9 rows. Rep eyelet row as for sleeve on 5th and 8th row. Place sts on holder. Rep for other side.

Neckband

K 6 sts from right front holder, pick up and k7 sts around right front neck, K18 sts from back neck holder, pick up and k 7 sts around left front neck, 6 sts from left front holder—44 sts. K 7 rows. Bind off.

Ties

With crochet hook and B, make 3 chains each approx 42"/106.5cm long. Lace through eyelets on placket and sleeve cuffs.

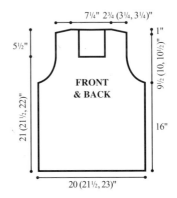

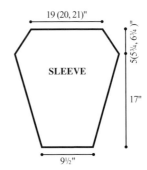

Thick cables add deep texture and dramatic flair to Vladimir Teriokhin's deliciously indulgent cashmere cap. Jaunty pom-poms provide playful panache.

■ Head circumference 19"/48.5cm

■ 2 1¾oz/50g balls (each approx 83yd/75m) Schulana/Skacel *Cashmere Tweed* (cashmere⑤) in #900 red
■ One pair size 10 (6mm) needles *or size to obtain gauge*
■ Size J/10 (6mm) crochet hook
■ Cable needle

14 sts and 16 rows to 4"/10cm over cable pats using size 10 (6mm) needles and 2 strands of yarn.
Take time to check gauge.

Note
Work with 2 strands of yarn held tog throughout.

Cr2R
Slip 1 st to cn and hold to *back*, k1, k1 from cn.
Cr2L
Slip 1 st to cn and hold to *front*, k1, k1 from cn.

Cr3R
Slip 1 st to cn and hold to *back*, k2, k1 from cn.
Cr3L
Slip 2 sts to cn and hold to *front*, k1, k2 from cn.
Cr4R
Slip 2 sts to cn and hold to *back*, k2, k2 from cn.

Cable #1
(over 8 sts)
Row 1 (RS) K4, Cr4R.
Rows 2, 4 and 6 Purl.
Row 3 K2, Cr4R, k2.
Row 5 Cr4R, k4.
Rep rows 1–6 for cable #1.

Cable #2
(over 4 sts)
Rows 1 and 3 (RS) Knit.
Rows 2, 4 and 6 Purl.
Row 5 Cr4R. Rep rows 1-6 for cable #2.

Cable #3
(over 8 sts)
Row 1 (RS) P2, Cr4R, p2.
Row 2 and all WS rows K the knit sts and p the purl sts.
Row 3 P1, Cr3R, Cr3L, p1.
Row 5 Cr3R, k2, Cr3L.
Row 7 Cr3L, k2, Cr3R.
Row 9 P1, Cr3L, Cr3R, p1.
Row 10 Rep row 2.
Rep rows 1–10 for cable #3.

HAT

With 2 strands of yarn, cast on 66 sts. Work in k1, p1 rib for 2 rows.

Beg cable pats

Next row (RS) *P2, work 8 sts cable #1, p2, work 4 sts cable #2, p2,work 8 sts cable #3, p2, work 4 sts cable #2; rep from * once more, p2. Cont in pats as established, work sts between cables in reverse St st, until piece measures 4"/10cm from beg, end with a WS row.

Top shaping

Next row (RS) Dec 1 st in each p2 section—57 sts. Work 3 rows even. **Next row (RS)** Dec 2 sts in each cable section—41 sts. Work 3 rows even, keeping to cable pat when possible, but working Cr2R and Cr2L in place of 3- and 4-st cables. **Next row (RS)** Dec 3 sts in each 6-st cable section—29 sts. Work 1 row even. Dec 9 sts evenly on next row—20 sts. Work 1 row even. K2tog across next row. Work 1 row even. K2tog across next row. Cut yarn, leaving an end for sewing. Draw through rem 5 sts and pull tog tightly. Sew back seam.

FINISHING

With 2 strands held tog and crochet hook, make two chains each approx 8"/20.5cm long and attach to top of hat. Make two 1"/2.5cm pom-poms and sew to end of each chain.

Teva Durham takes a new angle on argyle in this man's vest. Knit with a double strand of yarn to make it extra-chunky and extra-quick, this argyle adaptation is accentuated by duplicate-stitch diamonds.

SIZES

Instructions are written for Man's size Small. Changes for sizes Medium and Large are in parentheses.

KNITTED MEASUREMENTS

- Chest 40 (43, 46)"/101.5 (109, 117)cm
- Length 22½ (24, 25)"/57 (61, 63.5)cm

MATERIALS

- 4 (5, 6) 4oz/113g balls (each approx 125yd/114m) of Brown Sheep *Lamb's Pride Bulky* (wool/mohair⑤) in #M87 taupe (MC)
- 2 balls in #M47 teal (A)
- 1 ball in #M67 loden (B)
- Small amount of #M180 red (C) for duplicate st
- One pair size 15 (10mm) needles *or size to obtain gauge*
- Size P (15mm) crochet hook
- Tapestry needle

GAUGE

8 sts and 12 rows to 4"/10cm over St st using size 15 (10mm) needles.
Take time to check gauge.

Notes

1 Work with 2 strands of yarn held tog throughout.

2 When changing colors, twist yarns on WS to prevent holes.

3 For back, work RS chart rows from right to left, and WS chart rows from left to right. For front, work RS chart rows from left to right, and WS chart rows from right to left.

BACK

With size 15 (10mm) needles and 2 strands MC held tog, cast on 36 (39, 42) sts. Work in k1, p1 rib for 1½ "/4cm, inc 4 sts evenly across last WS row—40 (43, 46) sts. Beg chart for desired size, work as indicated through row 37 (37, 41).

Armhole shaping

Next row (RS) Bind off 2 sts at beg of next 2 rows, dec 1 st each side every other row 3 times—30 (33, 36) sts. Work even through chart row 63 (66, 70). Bind off all sts loosely.

FRONT

Work as for back until armhole measures 6½ (8, 7½)"/15 (20.5, 19)cm, end with a WS row.

Neck shaping

Next row (RS) Work 12 (13, 14) sts, join a 2nd ball of yarn and bind off center 6 (7, 8) sts, work to end. Working both sides at once, dec 1 st at each neck edge *every* row 4 times, then every other row twice. Bind off rem 6 (7, 8) sts each side for shoulders.

FINISHING

Block pieces to measurements. With tapestry needle and single strand C, work duplicate st following chart. Sew left shoulder seam.

Neckband

With RS facing and 2 strands MC, beg at left shoulder, pick up and k 16 (17, 18) sts along back neck, 5 sts along left side neck edge, 5 (6, 7) sts along center neck, 5 sts along right side neck—31 (33, 35) sts. Work in k1, p1 rib for 1½"/4cm. Bind off loosely (for cleaner edge, cut one strand yarn and bind off with single strand). Sew right shoulder seam and neckband seam. Sew side seams.

Armhole bands

With 2 strands MC and crochet hook, work 1 row sc around armholes (working into every other row).

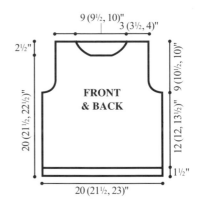

9 (9½, 10)"
3 (3½, 4)"
2½"
20 (21½, 22½)"
9 (10½, 10)"
FRONT & BACK
12 (12, 13½)"
1½"
20 (21½, 23)"

Color Key

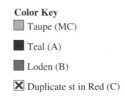

☐ Taupe (MC)

■ Teal (A)

■ Loden (B)

☒ Duplicate st in Red (C)

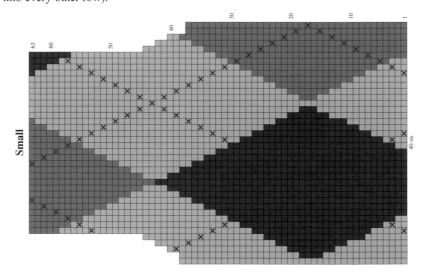

Small

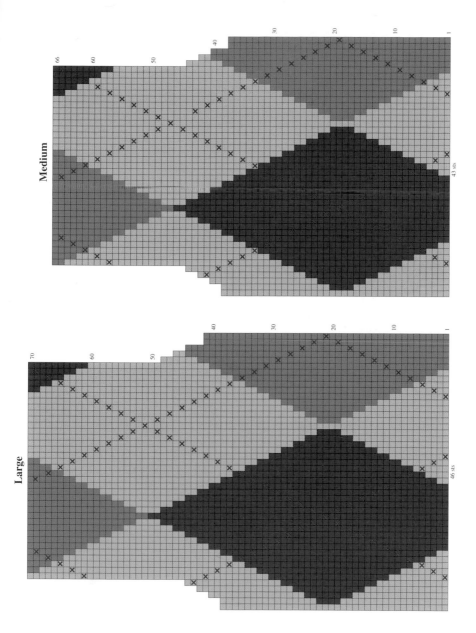

Medium

Large

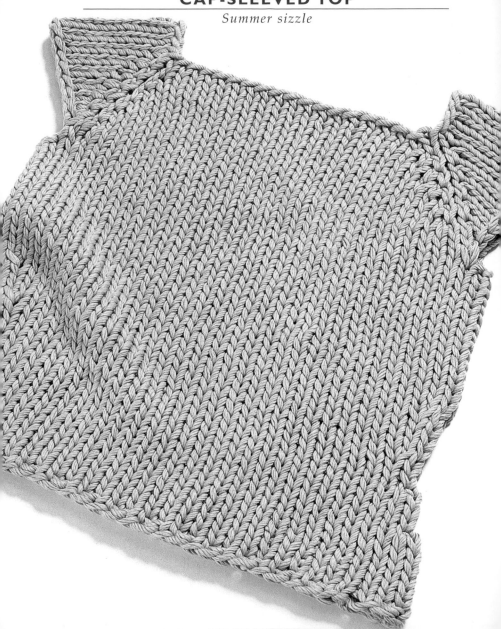

Light and lofty, Teva Durham's fitted cotton top is perfect for warm-weather wear. The square neck and raglan-style cap sleeves add a breezy touch to this summer essential.

SIZES

Instructions are written for size Small/Medium. Changes for size Medium/Large are in parentheses.

KNITTED MEASUREMENTS

- Bust 33 (37)"/84 (94)cm
- Length 16 (17)"/40.5 (43)cm
- Upper arm 10½ (12½)"/26.5 (32)cm

MATERIALS

- 4 (5) 3½oz/100g balls (each approx 51yd/47m) of Classic Elite *Weekend Cotton* (cotton ⑤) in #4835 green
- One size 15 (10mm) circular needle, 24"/60cm long *or size to obtain gauge*
- Stitch markers

GAUGE

8 sts and 12 rnds to 4"/10cm over St st using size 15 (10mm) needle.
Take time to check gauge.

Note

Sweater is worked in one piece, beg at neck and working from top down.

Inc 1

K into front and back of st.

BODY

With size 15 (10mm) needle, cast on 56 (64) sts. Join, taking care not to twist sts on needles. Place marker at beg of rnd and sl marker every rnd. K 2 rnds.
Rnd 3 *Inc 1, inc 1, k7 (9), inc 1, inc 1, k17 (19); rep from * around—64 (72) sts.
Rnd 4 and all even rnds through rnd 12 Knit.
Rnd 5 K1, inc 1, inc 1, k9 (11), inc 1, inc 1, k19 (21), inc 1, inc 1, k9 (11), inc 1, inc 1, k18 (20)—72 (80) sts.
Rnd 7 K2, inc 1, inc 1, k11 (13), inc 1, inc 1, k21 (23), inc 1, inc 1, k11 (13), inc 1, inc 1, k19 (21)—80 (88) sts.
Rnd 9 K3, inc 1, inc 1, k13 (15), inc 1, inc 1, k23 (25), inc 1, inc 1, k13 (15), inc 1 , inc 1, k20 (22)—88 (96) sts.
Rnd 11 K4, inc 1, inc 1, k15 (17), inc 1, inc 1, k25 (27), inc 1, inc 1, k15 (17), inc, 1, inc 1, k21 (23)—96 (104) sts.
Rnd 13 K7, bind off 18 (20) sts (sleeve), k30 (32) (front), bind off 18 (20) sts (sleeve), k23 (25) (back)—60 (64) sts.
Rnd 14 Make underarms as foll: K7, cast on 3 (5) sts, k30 (32) (front), cast on 3 (5) sts, k23 (25) (back)—66 (74) sts.
Rnds 15–29 Knit.
Rnd 30 (dec) K6, k2tog, k1, ssk, k28 (32), k2tog, k1, ssk, k22 (26)—62 (70) sts.
Rnds 31–33 Knit.

Rnd 34 (dec) K5, k2tog, k1, ssk, k26 (30), k2tog, k1, ssk, k21 (25)—58 (66) sts.

Rnds 35–37 Knit.

Rnd 38 (inc) K5, inc 1, inc 1, k27 (31), inc 1, inc 1, k22 (26)—62 (70) sts.

Rnds 39–41 Knit.

Rnd 42 (inc) K6, inc 1, inc 1, k29 (33), inc 1, inc 1, k23 (27)—66 (74) sts.

Rnds 43–48 Knit.

Size Medium/Large only Knit 3 rnds.

Both sizes Bind off loosely in k1, p1 rib.

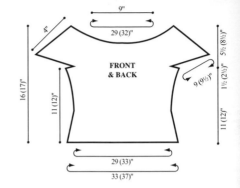

FRONT & BACK

9"

29 (32)"

4"

16 (17)"

11 (12)"

5½ (8½)"

1½ (2½)"

9 (9½)"

11 (12)"

29 (33)"

33 (37)"

STRIPED PILLOWS

From every angle

Diagonal stripes, two bold colorways, and a knobby bouclé ensure that these throw pillows will add a splash of color and texture to any décor. Designed by Carol Noble.

KNITTED MEASUREMENTS

■ 17" x 17"/43cm x 43cm square

MATERIALS

Tropical fruit pillow

■ 4 4oz/125g balls (each approx 70yds/64m) of Cherry Tree Hill Yarn *Andean Trail* (alpaca/wool⑥) in purple (A)

■ 2 balls in orange (B)

■ 1 each in gold (C), pale coral (D), orange-red (E), pale yellow green (F), loden green (G) and medium yellow (H)

Candies pillow

■ 4 balls in cerise (I)

■ 2 balls in orange (J)

■ 1 ball each in butter yellow (K), pale pink (L), mint green (M), turquoise (N), indigo (O), burgundy (P)

Both pillows

■ One pair size 11 (8mm) needles *or size to obtain gauge*

■ 16"/40cm square pillow form for each pillow

■ Size K/10½ (7mm) crochet hook

GAUGE

8 sts and 16 rows to 4"/10cm over garter st using size 11 (8mm) needles.
Take time to check gauge.

Note

Work in garter st using the intarsia method, with 2 strands of yarn held tog throughout.

PILLOWS

Tropical fruit pillow

Back

With color A, cast on 34 sts. Work in garter st for 17"/43cm. Bind off.

Front

Work in garter st and chart for colors as foll: Work rows 1–34 once, then rep rows 11–34 once more, then work last 8 rows of chart (66 rows in total). Bind off loosely.

Candies pillow

Back

With color I, cast on 34 sts. Work in garter st for 17"/43cm. Bind off.

Front

Work in garter st and chart as described in tropical fruit pillow. Bind off loosely.

FINISHING

With wrong sides together, work single crochet around 3 sides to join, using color B for tropical fruit pillow and color J for candies pillow. Slip in pillow insert. Work crochet along final side.

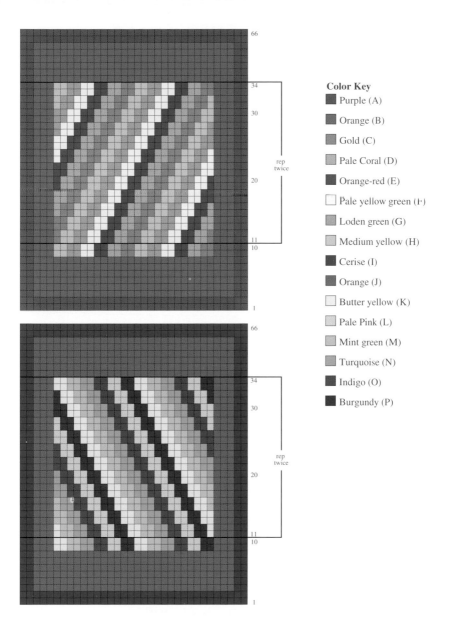

Color Key

- ■ Purple (A)
- ■ Orange (B)
- ■ Gold (C)
- ■ Pale Coral (D)
- ■ Orange-red (E)
- □ Pale yellow green (F)
- ■ Loden green (G)
- ■ Medium yellow (H)
- ■ Cerise (I)
- ■ Orange (J)
- □ Butter yellow (K)
- ■ Pale Pink (L)
- ■ Mint green (M)
- ■ Turquoise (N)
- ■ Indigo (O)
- ■ Burgundy (P)

Very Easy Very Vogue

A beaded rib stitch in Norah Gaughan's super-long turtleneck adds visual appeal and an extra-slim look. Simple dropped shoulders and thick alpaca yarn ensure a quick knit and luxurious feel.

SIZES

Instructions are written for size Small. Changes for sizes Medium and Large are in parentheses.

KNITTED MEASUREMENTS

■ Bust 42 (46, 50)"/106.5 (116.5, 127)cm
■ Length 26 (27, 28)"/66 (68.5, 71)cm
■ Upper arm 16½ (17, 17½)"/42 (43, 44.5)cm

MATERIALS

■ 10 (12, 13) 3½oz/100g balls (each approx 110yd/101m) of Reynolds/JCA *Andean Alpaca Regal* (alpaca⑤) in #17 turquoise
■ One pair size 10 (6mm) needles *or size to obtain gauge*
■ Sizes 8 and 10 (5mm and 6mm) circular needles, 16"/40cm long

GAUGE

14 sts and 20 rows to 4"/10cm over rib pat (slightly stretched) using larger needles. *Take time to check gauge.*

RIB PATTERN

(Back and forth)
Row 1 (WS) K1 *p2, k4; rep from * to last 3 sts, p2, k1.
Row 2 *K4, p2; rep from * to last 4 sts, k4.
Rep rows 1 and 2 for rib pat.

RIB PATTERN

(Circular)
Rnd 1 *K2, p4; rep from * to end.
Rnd 2 K3 *p2, k4; rep from * to last 3 sts, end p2, k1.
Rep rnds 1 and 2 for rib pat.

BACK

With larger needles, cast on 76 (82, 88) sts. Work back and forth in rib pat until piece measures 26 (27, 28)"/66 (68.5, 71)cm from beg. Bind off in pat.

FRONT

Work as for back until piece measures 24 (25, 26)"/61 (63.5, 66)cm from beg, end with a WS row.

Neck shaping
Next row (RS) K 30 (33, 36) sts, join 2nd ball of yarn and bind off center 16 sts, work to end. Working both sides at once, bind off from each neck edge 3 (3, 4) sts once, 2 (2, 3) sts once, 1 st once. Work even until piece measures same as back. Bind off 24 (27, 28) sts each side for shoulders.

SLEEVES

With larger needles, cast on 34 sts. Work back and forth in rib pat, AT SAME TIME, when piece measures 2"/5cm from beg, inc 1 st each side every 4th row 1 (3, 4) times, every 6th row 11 (10, 10) times—58 (60, 62) sts. Work even until piece measures 17 (17½, 18)"/43 (44.5, 45.5)cm from beg. Bind off in pat.

FINISHING

Block pieces to measurements. Sew shoulder seams.

Collar

With size 8 (5mm) circular needle, beg at center back neck, pick up 76 (82, 88) sts evenly around neck edge. K 1 rnd, inc 2 sts evenly around—78 (84, 90) sts. Work in rib pat (circular) for 3"/7.5cm. Change to size 10 (6mm) circular needle and cont in pat until collar measures 15"/38cm. Bind off in rib.

Place markers 8¼ (8½, 8¾)"/21 (21.5, 22)cm down from shoulder seams on front and back. Sew top of sleeves between markers. Sew side and sleeve seams.

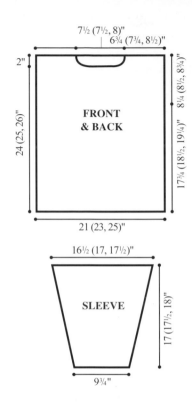

7½ (7½, 8)"
6¾ (7¾, 8½)"
2"
24 (25, 26)"
FRONT & BACK
8¼ (8½, 8¾)"
17¾ (18½, 19¼)"
21 (23, 25)"

16½ (17, 17½)"
SLEEVE
17 (17½, 18)"
9¾"

Rebecca Rosen's very simple turtleneck alternates stockinette and garter stripes. Two strands of yarn held together add texture to the body of the sweater; one strand in the turtleneck gives it a loose, draped look.

SIZES

Instructions are written for size Small. Changes for sizes Medium and Large are in parentheses.

KNITTED MEASUREMENTS

- Bust 36 (40, 44)"/91.5 (101.5, 112)cm
- Length 19½ (20, 20½)"/49 (50, 51.5)cm
- Upper arm 15 (16, 17)"/38 (40.5, 43)cm

MATERIALS

- 11 (13, 14) 1¾oz/50g balls (each approx 66yd/56m) of GGH/Muench Yarns *Venus* (mohair/nylon⑤) in #08 rust (A)
- 7 (8, 9) 3½oz/100g balls (each approx 100yd/90m) of Horstia/Muench Yarns *Mogador* (viscose/wool⑤) in #113 rust (B)
- One pair size 15 (10mm) needles *or size to obtain gauge*
- Size 13 (9mm) circular needle, 16"/40cm long

GAUGE

9 sts and 13 rows to 4"/10cm over garter st using one strand of A and one strand of B held tog and size 15 (10mm) needles. *Take time to check gauge.*

Notes

1 Sweater is worked holding one strand of each yarn tog throughout, except for the collar.

2 Sleeves are worked by picking up sts on body and working from top down.

BACK

With one strand of A and one strand of B held tog, cast on 42 (47, 52) sts. Work in St st for 5"/12.5cm. Change to garter st and work even until piece measures 10"/25cm from beg. Change to St st and work even until piece measures 15"/38cm from beg. Change to garter st and work even until piece measures 19½ (20, 20½)"/49 (50, 51.5)cm from beg. Bind off all sts.

FRONT

Work as for back.

SLEEVES

Block front and back to measurements. Place markers 5½ (6¼, 7¼)"/14 (16, 18.5)cm in from top edges on front and back and sew shoulder seams between edges and markers. Place markers 7½ (8, 8½)"/19 (20.5, 21.5)cm down from shoulder seams on front and back. With one strand of A and one strand of B held tog, pick up 36 (38, 40) sts between markers on one side. Work even in garter st for 3"/7.5cm. Dec 1 st each side of next row, then every 14th (14th, 12th) row 3 (3, 4) times more—28 (30, 30) sts. Work even until sleeve measures 19"/ 48.5cm from beg. Bind off all sts. Rep for other sleeve.

FINISHING
Block sleeves.

Cowl neck

With RS facing, circular needle and A, pick up 46 (48, 50) sts evenly around neck. Join and work in St st as foll: K 1 rnd. Inc 11 (12, 13) sts evenly around next rnd—57 (60, 63) sts. K 1 rnd. Inc 14 (14, 15) sts evenly around next rnd—71 (74, 78) sts. K 1 rnd. Inc 16 (16, 18) sts evenly around next rnd—87 (90, 96) sts. Cont in k2, p1 rib until cowl neck measures 9"/23cm. Bind off loosely in rib.
Sew side and sleeve seams.

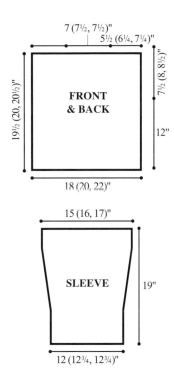

7 (7½, 7½)"

5½ (6¼, 7¼)"

7½ (8, 8½)"

FRONT & BACK

19½ (20, 20½)"

12"

18 (20, 22)"

15 (16, 17)"

SLEEVE

19"

12 (12¾, 12¾)"

HOUNDS-TOOTH

It's a dog's life

A **dapper houndstooth pattern gives your favorite pup a pedigreed look. Jean Guirguis's charming sweater is boldly checked in red and charcoal grey, then finished with a snug ribbed edging.**

SIZES

Instructions are written for one size.

KNITTED MEASUREMENTS

- Neck 10"/25.5cm
- Chest 14"/35.5cm
- Length 18"/46cm (neckband folded)

MATERIALS

- 2 170g/6oz balls (each approx 108yd/ 97m) of Lion Brand *Wool-Ease Thick & Quick* in #149 charcoal (A) and #113 scarlet (B)
- One pair each sizes 11 and 13 (8mm and 9mm) needles *or size to obtain gauge*
- Size 11 (8mm) circular needle, 24"/ 60cm long
- One set (4) dpn size 11 (8mm)
- Tapestry needle
- Stitch holder
- Bobbins

GAUGE

11 sts and 12 rows to 4"/10cm over St st and chart pat using larger needles. *Take time to check gauge.*

Note

When changing colors, twist yarn on WS to prevent holes, and carry unused yarn loosely across back of work.

BODY

With smaller needles and A, beg at neck and cast on 43 sts. **Row 1 (RS)** K1, *k1, p1; rep from * to last st, k1. **Row 2** K1, *p1, k1; rep from * to end. Rep last 2 rows until piece measures 5"/12.5cm from beg, end with a WS row. Change to larger needles. Work in St st and chart pat, inc 1 st each side (working inc sts into pat) on next row, then *every* row 4 times more— 53 sts. Work even until piece measures 8"/20.5cm from beg.

Leg openings

Working both legs at same time, k4, bind off 6 sts, k33, bind off 6 sts, k4—41 sts. Working with bobbins for each section, cont in pat until leg openings measure 4"/10cm, end with a WS row. **Next row (RS)** K4, cast on 6 sts, k33, cast on 6 sts, k4—53 sts. Cont in pat until piece measures 13"/33cm from beg (or until desired length to end of rib cage), end with a WS row.

Side edge shaping

Cont in pat, bind off 6 sts at beg of next 2 rows. **Next row (RS)** Ssk, work to last 2 sts, k2tog. Work 1 row even. Rep last 2 rows 4 times more—31 sts. Work even until piece measures 18½"/47cm (or until desired length to base of tail) from beg. Place sts on holder.

FINISHING
Block pieces to measurements. Join seam from neck edge to bound-off edge, reversing seam on neck for 2½"/6.5cm (for turnback turtleneck).

Back band
With RS facing, circular needle and A, beg at chest seam and pick up 18 sts evenly along edge to sts on holder, rib across sts, pick up 18 sts evenly along other edge to seam—67 sts. Join and work in k1, p1 rib for 4 rnds. Bind off loosely in rib.

Leg bands
With RS facing, dpn and A, pick up 32 sts evenly around leg opening. Join and work in k1, p1 rib for 5 rnds. Bind off loosely in rib.

Color Key
■ Charcoal (A)
■ Scarlet (B)

4-st rep

WEEKEND PULLOVER
Full tweed ahead!

Very Easy Very Vogue

Tweedy, hand-dyed yarn; bright, sophisticated colors; and a classic shape make this super-bulky pullover suitable for either a man or a woman. Designed by Susan Mills.

SIZES
Instructions are written for size X-Small. Changes for sizes Small, Medium, Large and X-Large are in parentheses.

KNITTED MEASUREMENTS
- Bust 37 (41, 44½, 48, 51½)"/94 (104, 113, 122, 130.5)cm
- Length 23½ (23½, 24, 24½, 25)"/59.5 (59.5, 61, 62, 63.5)cm
- Upper arm 19 (19, 19, 20½, 20½)"/48 (48, 48, 52, 52)cm

MATERIALS
- 6 (6, 6, 7, 7) 3½oz/100g balls (each approx 76yd/68m) of Artful Yarns/JCA *Museum* (wool⑥) in #2 bronze (MC)
- 2 balls each in #1 grey (A), #4 orange (C) and #6 green (E)
- 1 ball each in #3 purple (B) and #5 blue (D)
- One pair each sizes 11 and 13 (8mm and 9mm) needles *or size to obtain gauge*
- Size 11 (8mm) circular needle, 16"/40cm long
- Stitch holders

GAUGE
9 sts and 14 rows to 4"/10cm over St st using larger needles.
Take time to check gauge.

STITCH GLOSSARY
K2, P2 rib
(multiple of 4 sts plus 2)
Row 1 (RS) K2, *p2, k2; rep from * to end.
Row 2 P2, *k2, p2; rep from * to end.
Rep rows 1 and 2 for k2, p2 rib.

K2, P2 rib (in rnds)
(multiple of 4)
All rnds *K2, p2; rep from * around.

STRIPE PATTERN
2 rows C, 2 rows A, 6 rows B, 2 rows D, 2 rows MC, 4 rows A, 6 rows E, 2 rows C, 4 rows D, 6 rows MC, 2 rows A, 2 rows B, 2 rows C, 4 rows E, 2 rows A, 2 rows D, 4 rows B, 2 rows E, 2 rows C, 4 rows A, 2 rows MC.

BACK
With smaller needles and MC, cast on 42 (46, 50, 54, 58) sts. Work in k2, p2 rib for 6 (6, 8, 8, 10) rows. Change to larger needles and cont in St st for 2 (2, 2, 4, 4) rows. Work 64 rows stripe pat. Cont in St st with MC only until piece measures 22½ (22½, 23, 23½, 24)"/57 (57, 58.5, 59.5, 61)cm from beg, end with a WS row.
Neck shaping
Next row (RS) K12 (14, 16, 17, 19), place center 18 (18, 18, 20, 20) sts on holder for neck, join 2nd ball of yarn and work to end. Working both sides at once,

work 1 row even, then dec 1 st at each neck edge once. Bind off rem 11 (13, 15, 16 18) sts each side for shoulders.

FRONT

Work as for back until piece measures 21¼ (21¼, 21¾, 22¼, 22¾)"/54 (54, 55.5, 56.5, 58)cm from beg, end with a WS row.

Neck shaping

Next row (RS) K15 (17, 19, 20, 22), place center 12 (12, 12, 14, 14) sts on holder for neck, join 2nd ball of yarn and work to end. Working both sides at once, dec 1 st at each neck edge *every* row 4 times—11 (13, 15, 16, 18) sts each side. Work even until same length as back. Bind off sts each side for shoulders.

SLEEVES

With smaller needles and MC, cast on 26 (26, 26, 30, 30) sts. Work in k2, p2 rib for 8 rows, inc 1 (1, 1, 0, 0) st on last row— 27 (27, 27, 30, 30) sts. Change to larger needles and cont in St st, inc 1 st each side every 6th row 6 (6, 6, 4, 4) times, then every 8th row 2 (2, 2, 4, 4) times—43 (43, 43, 46, 46) sts. Work even until piece measures 18 (18, 18, 19, 19)"/45.5 (45.5, 45.5, 48, 48)cm from beg. Bind off.

FINISHING

Block pieces to measurements. Sew shoulder seams.

Neckband

With RS facing, circular needle and MC,

pick up 48 (48, 48, 52, 52) sts evenly around neck edge, including sts from holders. Join and work in k2, p2 rib for 2"/5cm. Bind off loosely in rib. Place markers 9½ (9½, 9½, 10¼, 10¼)"/24 (24, 24, 26, 26)cm down from shoulder seams on front and back. Sew top of sleeves between armohles. Sew side and sleeve seams.

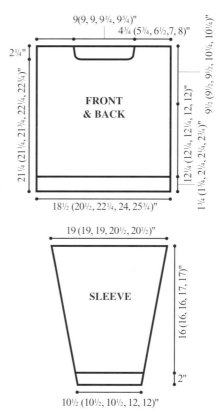

9(9, 9, 9¾, 9¾)"

4¾ (5¾, 6½, 7, 8)"

2¼"

21¼ (21¼, 21¾, 22¼, 22¾)"

FRONT & BACK

9½ (9½, 9½, 10¼, 10¼)"

12¼ (12¼, 12¼, 12, 12)"

1¾ (1¾, 2, 2¼, 2¾)"

18½ (20½, 22¼, 24, 25¾)"

19 (19, 19, 20½, 20½)"

SLEEVE

16(16, 16, 17, 17)"

2"

10½ (10½, 10½, 12, 12)"

Very Easy Very Vogue

Keep essentials handy in this clever handbag, designed by Gayle Bunn. Dimensional cables on a kangaroo pocket, wooden handles, and a neat fringe finish the look.

KNITTED MEASUREMENTS

10½" x 12"/26.5cm x 30.5cm

MATERIALS

■ 2 1¾oz/50g balls (each approx 80yd/73m) Patons® *Shetland Chunky* (acrylic/wool⑤) in #2178 blue
■ One pair size 10 (6mm) needles *or size to obtain gauge*
■ Cable needle
■ Wooden handles

GAUGE

15 sts and 20 rows to 4"/10cm over St st using size 10 (6mm) needles.
Take time to check gauge.

STITCH GLOSSARY

Cr5

Slip 4 sts onto cn and hold to *back*, k1, sl last 3 sts from cn to LH needle, bring cn to *front*, k3 from LH needle, k1 from cn.

FRONT AND BACK

(make 2 pieces)
Cast on 41 sts. Work in St st for 8½"/21.5cm, end with a WS row.

Shape top

Next row (RS) K2, k2tog, k to last 4 sts, ssk, k2. **Next row** Purl. Rep last 2 rows 4 times more—31 sts. **Next row (RS)** Knit. **Next row (WS)** Knit (for fold line). Beg with a k row, work 6 rows more in St st. Bind off.

Pocket

Cast on 36 sts.
Row I (WS) P2, *k2, p4; rep from * to last 4 sts, k2, p2. **Row 2** K2, *p2, k2, M1, k2; rep from * to last 4 sts, p2, k2—41 sts. **Row 3** P2, *k2, p5; rep from * to last 4 sts, k2, p2. **Row 4** K2, *P2, Cr5; rep from * to last 4 sts, p2, k2. **Row 5** Rep row 3. **Row 6** K2, *p2, k5; rep from * to last 4 sts, p2, k2. **Row 7** Rep row 3. **Row 8** Rep row 6. Rep rows 3-8 for pat and work 9 rows more.

Top shaping

Next row (RS) K1, ssk, work to last 3 sts, k2tog, k1. **Next row** P2, *k2, p1, p2tog, p2; rep from * to last 4 sts, k2, p2—24 sts. Bind off in pat.

FINISHING

Sew pocket to front, leaving top shaping open. Sew side and lower edge seams, leaving sides above top shaping open. Place handles in position and fold top of bag to inside along fold line. Sew facing to WS of bag. Cut 7½"/19cm lengths of yarn and, holding 3 strands tog, knot into fringe across lower edge. Trim fringe evenly.

CHILD'S CABLED JACKET

Zipity-doo-dah

Details reign in this cozy zippered jacket: a large, intricate cable design dominates the front while ribs and baby cables embellish the back and sleeves. A wide, ribbed waist and collar and a playful pom-pom provide all the trimmings. Designed by Mari Lynn Patrick.

SIZES

Instructions are written for Girl's size 8. Changes for sizes 10 and 12 are in parentheses.

KNITTED MEASUREMENTS

- Chest 33 (36, 38½)"/84 (91.5, 98)cm
- Length 16 (16, 18)"/40.5 (40.5, 45.5)cm
- Upper arm 11½ (12, 12½)"/29 (30.5, 32)cm

MATERIALS

- 10 (12 , 14) 1¾oz/50g balls (each approx 50yd/47m) of Naturally/S.R. Kertzer *Tibet* (wool/elastene⑥) in #04 green
- One pair each sizes 13 and 15 (9mm and 10mm) needles *or size to obtain gauge*
- One 14 (14, 16)"/35 (35, 40)cm separating zipper
- Size K/10½ (7mm) crochet hook

GAUGE

12 sts and 16 rows to 4"/10cm over rib and cable st (for back) using larger needles. *Take time to check gauge.*

STITCH GLOSSARY
C2R
Sl 1 st to cn and hold to *back*, k1, k1 from cn.

C4L
Sl 2 sts to cn and hold to *front*, k2, k2 from cn.
C4R
Sl 2 sts to cn and hold to *back*, k2, k2 from cn.
C3L
Sl 2 sts to cn and hold to *front*, k1, k2 from cn.
C3R
Sl 1 st to cn and hold to *back*, k2, k1 from cn.

BACK

With smaller needles, cast on 52 (56, 60) sts
Row 1 (RS) P1 (selvage st), beg with k2, (p2, k2), work in k2, p2 rib across, end with k2 (p2, k2), p1 (selvage st). Cont in rib as established for 2½"/6.5cm. Change to larger needles.

Beg rib and cable st chart
Row 1 (RS) P1 (selvage st), beg with st 5 (3, 1), work to rep line, then work 12-st rep across, end with st 18 (20, 22), p1 (selvage st). Cont to foll chart in this way until piece measures 9½ (9, 10½)"/24 (23, 26.5)cm from beg.

Armhole shaping
Bind off 3 sts at beg of next 2 rows, 2 sts at beg of next 2 rows, dec 1 st each side every other row 2 (3, 4) times—38 (40, 42) sts. Work even until armhole measures 5½ (6, 6½)"/14 (15, 16.5)cm.

Neck and shoulder shaping
Next row (RS) Work 14 (15, 15) sts, join a 2nd ball of yarn and bind off center 10 (10, 12) sts, work to end. Work both sides at once for 1 row more. Then cont to shape neck binding off 3 sts from each neck edge once, AT SAME TIME, binding off 5 (6, 6) sts from each shoulder edge once, 6 sts once.

LEFT FRONT

With smaller needles, cast on 25 (27, 29) sts.

Row I (RS) P1 (selvage st), beg with p2 (k2, p2), work in k2, p2 rib end with k2.

Row 2 Sl 1, p1, *k2, p2; rep from *, end k2 (p2, k2), k1 (selvage st). Cont to work in this way until rib measures 2½"/6.5cm. Change to larger needles.

Beg cable panel

Row I (RS) P9 (11, 13) (including selvage st), k12 (for cable panel), p3, k1.

Next row (WS) Sl 1 (for front selvage st), k3, p12 (cable panel), k9 (11, 13). Cont to work in this way through row 18 of chart then rep rows 7-18 for cable panel until piece measures same as back to armhole.

Armhole shaping

From armhole edge, bind off 3 sts once, 2 sts once, dec 1 st every other row 2 (3, 4) times—18 (19, 20) sts. Work even until armhole measures 4½ (5, 5½)"/11.5 (12.5, 14)cm.

Neck shaping

Next row (WS) Bind off 3 (3, 4) sts, work to end. Cont to shape neck binding off from neck edge 2 sts once, dec 1 st every other row twice—11 (12, 12) sts. When same length as back, bind off 5 (6, 6) sts from shoulder edge once, 6 sts once.

RIGHT FRONT

Work to correspond to left front, reversing pat placement and all shaping and sl first st at beg of RS rows for center front edge.

SLEEVES

Note Sleeves are worked in k2, p2 rib with one 2-st cable (C2R) worked on center 2 sts only.

With smaller needles, cast on 20 (24, 24) sts.

Row I (RS) P1 (3, 3), *k2, p2; rep from * end k2, p1 (3, 3).

Row 2 K the knit and p the purl sts.

Row 3 Rib 9 (11, 11) sts, C2R, rib 9 (11, 11) sts.

Row 4 Work even. Cont to work in this way, working C2R on center 2 sts every 4th row and inc 1 st each side on next row and every 4th row 7 (6, 7) times more—36 (38, 40) sts. Work even until piece measures 12 (13, 14½)"/30.5 (33, 37)cm from beg.

Cap shaping

Bind off 3 sts at beg of next 2 rows, 2 sts at beg of next 2 rows, dec 1 st each side every other row 6 (7, 8) times—14 sts. Bind off.

Block pieces to measurements. Sew shoulder seams.

Collar

With smaller needles, from WS pick up and k 46 (46, 50) sts evenly around neck edge.

Row I (WS of collar) P2, *k2, p2; rep from * to end. Cont in k2, p2 rib until collar measures 1"/2.5cm. Change to larger needles.

Next row (RS) K2, M1 k-st, rib to last 2 sts, M1 k-st, k2. Work 1 row even. Rep last 2 rows once.

Next row K2, M1 p-st, rib to last 2 sts, M1 p-st, k2. Work 1 row even. Rep last 2 rows once more—54 (54, 58) sts. Work even in rib until collar measures 3½"/9cm. Bind off in rib. Sew sleeves into armholes. Sew side and sleeve seams. Tack zipper in place, then sew in under the k1 selvage st. Make a 2"/5cm pom-pom. With crochet hook, ch 7, sl st in each ch and attach to pom-pom. Sew chain and pom pom to zipper pull with thread.

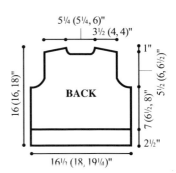

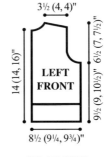

Stitch Key

☐ K on RS, p on WS

⊟ P on RS, k on WS

C2R

C3L

C3R

C4L

C4R

Cable Panel

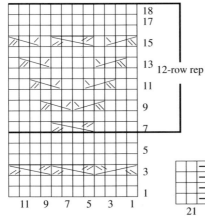

Rib and Cable Stitch

EASY SLEEVELESS TURTLENECK

Fitness fanatic

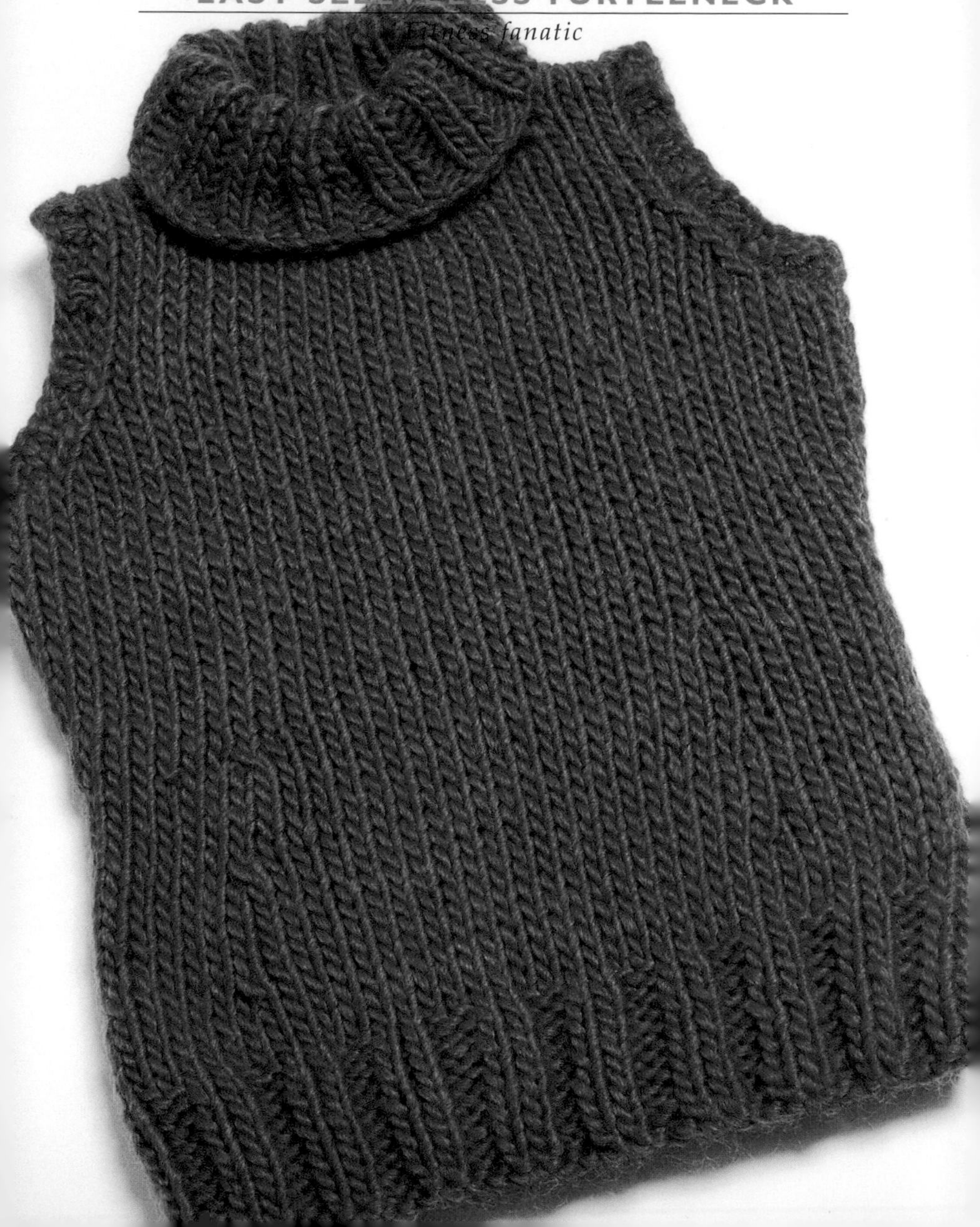

Sleek shaping steals center stage in this sleeveless top, designed by Mari Lynn Patrick. Interior full-fashioning creates the fitted shape, finished with ribbed trim at the armholes and hem.

SIZES
Instructions are written for size Small. Changes for sizes Medium and Large are in parentheses.

KNITTED MEASUREMENTS
- Bust 34 (35½, 37)"/86 (90, 94)cm
- Length 21½ (22, 22½)"/54.5 (56, 57)cm

MATERIALS
- 5 (5, 6) 3½oz/100g balls (each approx 55yd/51m) of Cleckheaton/Plymouth Yarns *Gusto10* (acrylic/wool/mohair⑥) in #2090 orange
- One pair each sizes 13 and 15 (9mm and 10mm) needles *or size to obtain gauge*
- Size 13 (9mm) circular needle, 16"/40cm long

GAUGE
9 sts and 12 rows to 4"/10cm over St st using larger needles.
Take time to check gauge.

BACK
With smaller needles, cast on 37 (41, 45) sts.
Row 1 (WS) P1, *k2, p2; rep from * to end.

Row 2 K the knit and p the purl sts. Cont in k2, p2 rib for 10 rows or 3"/7.5cm, inc 1 (dec 1, dec 3) sts on last RS row—38 (40, 42) sts. Change to larger needles. Beg with a p row, work in St st for 5 rows.
Dec row (RS) K7 (8, 9), pm, SKP, k to last 9 (10, 11) sts, k2tog, pm, k to end. Rep dec row every 6th row (working SKP after first marker and k2tog before 2nd marker) twice more—32 (34, 36) sts. Work even until piece measures 9½"/24cm from beg. Inc 1 st each side of next row then rep inc every 4th row once, every 6th row once— 38 (40, 42) sts. Work even until piece measures 14½"/37cm from beg.
Armhole shaping
Bind off 4 sts at beg of next 2 rows, dec 1 st each side every other row 3 times—24 (26, 28) sts. Work even until armhole measures 6 (6½, 7)"/15 (16.5, 18)cm.
Neck and shoulder shaping
Bind off 2 (3, 3) sts at beg of next 2 rows, 2 (2, 3) sts at beg of next 2 rows. Bind off center 16 sts.

FRONT
Work as for back until armhole measures 3 (3½, 4)"/7.5 (9, 10)cm.
Neck shaping
Next row (RS) K9 (10, 11) sts, join a 2nd ball of yarn and bind off center 6 sts, work to end. Working both sides at once, bind off 2 sts from each neck edge twice, 1 st once—4 (5, 6) sts rem each side. When same length as back, bind off 2 (3, 3) sts from armhole edge once, 2 (2, 3) sts once.

FINISHING

Block pieces to measurements. Sew shoulder seams.

Armhole bands

With smaller needles, pick up and k 38 (42, 46) sts evenly around armhole edge. Work in k2, p2 rib for 1 row. Bind off in rib.

Neckband

With smaller needles, pick up and k 48 sts evenly around neck edge. Work in k2, p2 rib for 6"/15cm. Bind off in rib. Sew side seams.

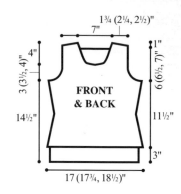

Fun details like a kangaroo pocket and bobbles add to the cozy charm of Gayle Bunn's child's set. A cowl neck tops the sweatshirt, and a twisted-cord tie keeps the hat secure.

SIZES

Instructions are written for Child's size 4. Changes for sizes 6, 8 and 10 are in parentheses.

KNITTED MEASUREMENTS

- Chest 29 (31, 33, 36)"/73.5 (78.5, 83.5, 91.5)cm
- Length 17 (18½, 20, 21½)"/43 (47, 50.5, 54.5)cm
- Upper arm 11 (11½, 12½, 13½)"/28 (29, 31.5, 34)cm

MATERIALS

Sweatshirt
- 8 (9, 10, 11) 1¾oz/50g balls (each approx 80yd/73m) of Patons® *Shetland Chunky* (acrylic/wool⑤) in #2308 purple

Hat
- 2 balls in #2308 purple
- One pair each sizes 9 and 10 (5.5mm and 6mm) needles *or size to obtain gauge*
- Stitch holders
- Cable needle

GAUGE

15 sts and 20 rows to 4"/10cm over St st using larger needles.
Take time to check gauge.

BACK

With smaller needles, cast on 55 (58, 61, 67) sts.

Row 1 (RS) *K2, p1; rep from * to last st, end k1.

Row 2 *P1, k2; rep from * to last st, end p1. Rep these 2 rows for rib pat 3 times more, inc 0 (1, 2, 0) sts evenly across last row—55 (59, 63, 67) sts. Change to larger needles and cont in St st until piece measures 10½ (11½, 12½, 13½)"/26.5 (29, 31.5, 34)cm from beg, end with a WS row.

Armhole shaping
Bind off 4 (4, 5, 5) sts beg of next 2 rows.

Next row (RS) K2, k2tog, k to last 4 sts, SKP, k2.

Next row Purl. Rep last 2 rows 2 (3, 3, 4) times more—41 (43, 45, 47) sts. Work even until armhole measures 6 (6½, 7, 7½)"/15 (16.5, 17.5, 19)cm, end with a WS row.

Shoulder shaping
Bind off 5 (5, 6, 6) sts beg of next 2 rows. Leave rem 31 (33, 33, 35) sts on a holder.

FRONT

Work as for back until armhole measures 4½ (4½, 5, 5)"/11.5 (11.5, 12.5, 12.5)cm, end with a WS row.

Neck shaping
Next row (RS) K10 (10, 11, 11) sts, place center 21 (23, 23, 25) sts on a holder, join 2nd ball of yarn and work to end. Working both sides at once, dec 1 st from each neck edge *every* row 5 times. Work even on rem 5 (5, 6, 6) sts each side until same length as back to shoulder. Bind off.

SLEEVES

With smaller needles, cast on 40 (40, 43, 46) sts. Work 18 rows in rib pat as for back, dec 3 (3, 2, 3) sts evenly across last row—37 (37, 41, 43) sts. Change to larger needles and cont in St st, inc 1 st each side on next row, then every 10th (10th, 12th, 12th) row 1 (2, 2, 3) times more—41 (43, 47, 51) sts. Work even until piece measures 11½ (13, 14½, 15½)"/29 (33, 37, 39.5)cm from beg, end with a WS row.

Cap shaping

Bind off 2 (2, 3, 3) sts beg of next 2 rows.

Next (dec) row (RS) K2, k2tog, k to last 4 sts, ssk, k2.

Next row Purl. Rep last 2 rows 5 (8, 9, 9) times more—25 (21, 21, 25) sts.

Next (dec) row (RS) K2, k2 tog, k to last 4 sts, ssk, k2.

Next (dec) row P2, p2 tog tbl, p to last 4 sts, p2tog, p2. Rep last 2 rows until there are 9 sts. Bind off.

POCKET

With larger needles, cast on 41 (41, 45, 45) sts. Work in St st until piece measures 3 (3, 3½, 3½)"/7.5 (7.5, 9, 9)cm from beg, end with a WS row. **Next (dec) row (RS)** K2, k2tog, k to last 4 sts, ssk, k2. Work 3 rows even. Rep last 4 rows 3 (3, 4, 4) times more, then work dec row once more—31 (31, 33, 33) sts. P 1 row. Bind off.

FINISHING

Block pieces to measurements. Sew right shoulder seam. Sew pocket to front as shown in photo.

Collar

With RS facing and larger needles, pick up and k 7 (8, 8, 9) sts down left front neck edge, k21 (23, 23, 25) sts from front holder, pick up and k 7 (8, 8, 9) sts up right front neck edge, k31 (33, 33, 35) from back holder—66 (72, 72, 78) sts. **Next row (WS)** Knit. Cont in St st until collar measures 4¾ (5¼, 5¼, 5½)"/12 (13.5, 13.5, 14)cm, end with a RS row. K 4 rows. Bind off knitwise. Sew left shoulder and collar seam. Set in sleeves. Sew side and sleeve seams.

HAT

STITCH GLOSSARY

MB (make bobble)

Knit into front, back, front and back of next st. Turn. Sl 1, p3. Turn. Sl 1, k3. Turn. Sl 1, p3. Turn. Sl 4, pass first 3 sts over 4th st, k1.

C6B

Slip 3 sts to cn and hold to *back*, k3, k3 from cn.

C4B

Slip 2 sts to cn and hold to *back*, k2, k2 from cn.

First ear flap

With larger needles, cast on 3 sts. **Row 1 (WS)** P1, k1, p1. **Row 2** K1, M1, p1, M1, k1. **Row 3** P1, k3, p1. **Row 4** K1, M1, p1, MB, p1, M1, k1. **Row 5** P2, k3, p2. **Row 6** K1, M1, k1, p3, k1, M1, k1. **Row 7** P3, k3, p3. **Row 8** K1, M1, k2, p3, k2, M1, k1. **Row 9** P4, k3, p4. **Row 10** K1, M1, k3, p3, k3, M1, k1. **Row 11** P5, k3, p5. **Row 12** K1, M1, k4, p1, MB, p1, k4, M1, k1.

Row 13 P6, k3, p6. **Row 14** K1, M1, k5, p3, k5, M1, k1. **Row 15** P7, k3, p7. **Row 16** K1, M1, k6, p3, k6, M1, k1. **Row 17** P1, k1, p6, k3, p6, k1, p1—19 sts. Cut yarn and leave sts on holder.

Second ear flap

Work as for first ear flap, but do not cut yarn and cont as foll:

Body of hat

With RS facing, cast on 9 sts. P2, k6, p1 across these 9 sts, p2, k6, p3, k6, p2 across second ear flap. Turn and cast on 26 sts. Turn and p2, k6, p3, k6, p2 across first ear flap. Turn and cast on 9 sts—82 sts. **Next row (WS)** K2, *p6, k3; rep from * to last 8 sts, p6, k2. Cont in pat as foll:

Row 1 P2, *C6B, p1, MB, p1; rep from * to last 8 sts, C6B, p2. **Rows 2, 4 and 6** K2, *p6, k3; rep from * to last 8 sts, p6, k2.

Rows 3, 5 and 7 P2, *k6, p3; rep from * to last 8 sts, k6, p2. **Row 8** Rep row 2.

Rows 9–16 Rep last 8 rows once more.

Row 17 Rep row 1. **Row 18** K2, *p2, p2tog, p2, k3; rep from * to last 8 sts, p2, p2tog, p2, k2—73 sts. **Row 19** P2, *k5, p3; rep from * to last 7 sts, k5, p2. **Row 20** K2, *p5, k3; rep from * to last 7 sts, p5, k2. **Row 21** Rep row 19. **Row 22** K2, *p2, p2tog, p1, k3; rep from * to last 7 sts, p2, p2tog, p1, k2—64 sts. **Row 23** P2, *k4, p3; rep from * to last 6 sts, k4, p2. **Row 24** K2tog, *p4, k3tog; rep from * to last 6 sts, p4, k2tog—54 sts. **Row 25** P1, *C4B, MB; rep from * to last 5 sts, C4B, p1. **Row**

26 Purl. **Row 27** *K2, k2tog; rep from * to last 2 sts, k2—41 sts. **Row 28** Purl. **Row 29** *K1, k2tog; rep from * to last 2 sts, k2—28 sts. **Row 30** Purl. **Row 31** K2tog across—14 sts. **Row 32** [P2, p2tog] 3 times, p2—11 sts.

Work 6 rows even in St st. Cut yarn, leaving a long end. Draw end through rem sts tightly and fasten. Sew center back seam. With 3 strands of yarn, make two 12"/30.5cm long twisted cords and join to end of each ear flap.

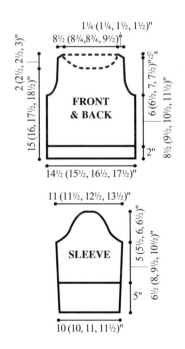

14½ (15½, 16½, 17½)"

8½ (8¾, 8¾, 9½)"

1¼ (1¼, 1½, 1½)"

2 (2½, 2½, 3)"

15 (16, 17½, 18½)"

½"

6 (6½, 7, 7½)"

8½ (9½, 10½, 11½)"

FRONT & BACK

2"

11 (11½, 12½, 13½)"

10 (10, 11, 11½)"

5 (5½, 6, 6½)"

6½ (8, 9½, 10½)"

5"

SLEEVE

The multicolored effect of this classic turtleneck is created by four strands of yarn—in different colors—knit together as one. The result is a rich blend that knits up in a snap. Designed by Veronica Manno.

SIZES

Instructions are written for size X-Small. Changes for sizes Small/Medium, and Large are in parentheses.

KNITTED MEASUREMENTS

- Bust 33 (41, 49)"/84 (104, 124.5)cm
- Length 18 (18½, 19½)"/46 (47,49.5)cm
- Upper arm 16 (17, 18½)"/40.5 (43, 47)cm

MATERIALS

- 5 (5, 6) 1¾oz/50g balls (each approx 136yd/125m) of Filatura Di Crosa/ Tahki• Stacy Charles, Inc. *Zara* each in #1449 red, #1498 gold, #1514 coral and #1501 pink
- One pair size 11 (8mm) needles *or size to obtain gauge*
- Size 11 (8mm) circular needle, 16"/ 40cm long

GAUGE

10 sts and 15 rows to 4"/10cm over St st using size 11 (8mm) needles and 4 strands (see note).
Take time to check gauge.

Note

Use 1 strand of each color (4 strands total) held tog throughout.

BACK

With 1 strand of each color held tog, cast on 42 (52, 62) sts. Work in k1, p1 rib for 1"/2.5cm. Cont in St st until piece measures 10 (10, 10½)"/25.5 (25.5, 26.5)cm from beg.

Armhole shaping

Bind off 3 sts at beg of next 0 (2, 2) rows, 2 sts at beg of next 2 (2, 4) rows, 1 st at beg of next 2 rows—36 (40, 46) sts. Work even until armhole measures 8 (8½, 9)"/20.5 (21.5, 23)cm. Bind off all sts.

FRONT

Work as for back until armhole measures 5½ (6, 6½)"/14 (15, 16.5)cm, end with a WS row.

Neck shaping

Next row (RS) Work 13 (15, 18) sts, join 2nd ball of yarn and bind off center 10 sts, work to end. Working both sides at once, bind off from each neck edge 2 sts twice, 1 st once. Work even until same length as back. Bind off rem 8 (10, 13) sts each side for shoulders.

SLEEVES

With 1 strand of each color held tog, cast on 22 (22, 24) sts. Work in k1, p1 rib for 1"/2.5cm, end with a WS row. Cont in St st, inc 1 st each side on next row, then every 4th row 0 (1, 4) times, every 6th row 8 (8, 6) times—40 (42, 46) sts. Work even until piece measures 17 (17½, 17½)"/43 (44.5, 44.5)cm from beg.

Cap shaping
Bind off 3 sts at beg of next 2 rows, 2 sts at beg of next 2 rows, dec 1 st each side every other row 5 (6, 7) times, bind off 4 sts at beg of next 2 rows, 3 sts at beg of next 2 rows. Bind off rem 6 (6, 8) sts

FINISHING
Block pieces to measurements. Sew shoulder seams.

Neckband
With RS facing, circular needle and 1 strand each color, pick up and k 50 sts evenly around neck edge. Join and work in k1, p1 rib for 7"/17.5cm. Bind off in rib. Set in sleeves. Sew side and sleeve seams.

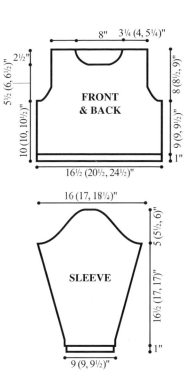

8"   3¼ (4, 5¼)"

2½"

5½ (6, 6½)"

FRONT & BACK

8 (8½, 9)"

9 (9, 9½)"

10 (10, 10½)"

16½ (20½, 24½)"

1"

16 (17, 18½)"

5 (5½, 6)"

SLEEVE

16½ (17, 17)"

9 (9, 9½)"

1"

EASY SCARF
Express lane

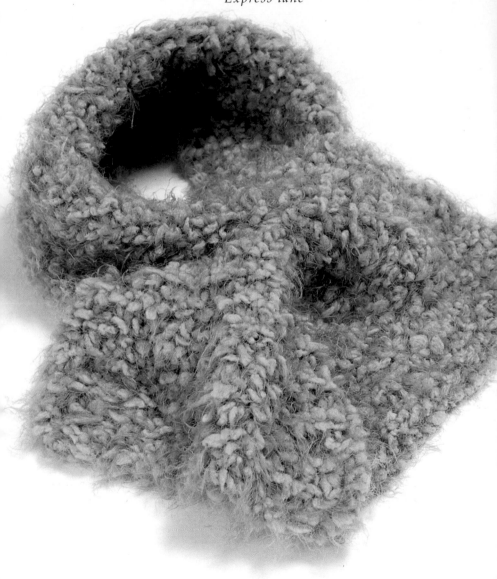

Very Easy Very Vogue

Trisha Malcolm's pull-through scarf provides the perfect recipe for a first project: simple garter stitch, a bind off for the cross over, and an easy color change. A doubled strand of fuzzy yarns offers instant gratification to the novice knitter.

KNITTED MEASUREMENTS
Length 30"/76cm

MATERIALS
- 1 1¾oz/50g balls (each approx 72yd/65m) Trendsetter *Zucca* (tactel/nylon⑤) in #5042 turquoise (A-1) and #5135 lime green (B-1)
- 1 1¾oz/50g hanks (each approx 180yd/162m) Trendsetter *Voila* (nylon④) in #42 turquoise (A-2) and #23 lime green (B-2)
- One pair size 15 (10mm) needles *or size to obtain gauge*

GAUGE
10 sts to 4"/10cm over garter st using size 15 (10mm) needles and 1 strand each of *Zucca* and *Voila* held tog.
Take time to check gauge.

Note
Work with 1 strand each of *Zucca* and *Voila* held tog throughout.

SCARF
With 1 strand each of A-1 and A-2 held tog, cast on 20 sts. Work in garter st for 5"/12.5cm.
Next row K7, bind off 6 sts, k to end. On next row, cast on 6 sts over bound-off sts. Work even until piece measures 15"/38cm from beg. Change to B-1 and B-2 held tog and cont in garter st for 15"/38cm more. Bind off.

Two wide, braided cable panels add the crowning touch to this high-necked pullover, designed by Barbara Khouri. Raglan sleeves and thick-and-thin yarn add extra interest to a classic style.

SIZES

Instructions are written for size Small. Changes for sizes Medium and Large are in parentheses.

KNITTED MEASUREMENTS

- Bust 38 (42, 46)"/96.5 (106.5, 117)cm
- Length 23 (23½, 24)"/58.5 (59.5, 61)cm
- Upper Arm 14 (15, 16¾)"/35.5 (38, 42.5)cm

MATERIALS

- 8 (9, 10) 1¾oz/100g balls (each approx 93yd/85m) of Reynolds/JCA *Allagash* (wool⑥) in #645 iris
- One pair each sizes 9 and 10½ (5.5mm and 6.5mm) needles *or size to obtain gauge*
- Size 9 (5.5mm) circular needle, 16"/40cm long
- Cable needle
- Stitch holders

GAUGE

11 sts and 16 rows to 4"/10cm over St st using larger needles.
Take time to check gauge.

Note

Selvage sts are included in instructions, but not in final measurements.

Cable pattern

(over 18 sts)

Row 1 and all WS rows K2, [p2, k1] 4 times, p2, k2.

Rows 2 and 6 P2, [k2, p1], 4 times, k2, p2.

Row 4 P2, k2, [p1, sl 3 sts to cn and hold to *front* of work, k2, sl the p st back to LH needle and purl it, k2 from cn] twice, p2.

Row 8 P2, [sl 3 sts to cn and hold to *back* of work, k2, sl the p st back to LH needle and purl it, k2 from cn, p1] twice, k2, p2.

Rep rows 1–8 for cable pat.

BACK

With larger needles, cast on 72 (76, 82) sts.

Establish pat

Row 1 (WS) P15 (17, 20), work cable pat over next 18 sts, p6, work cable pat over next 18 sts, p15 (17, 20). Cont as established, working sts outside of cable pat in St st, until piece measures 14½ (14½, 14)"/37 (37, 35.5)cm from beg, end with a WS row.

Raglan armhole shaping

Bind off 2 sts at beg of next 2 rows. **Next (dec) row (RS)** K1, ssk, work to last 3 sts, k2tog, k1. Work 1 row even. Rep last 2 rows 15 (16, 18) times more, AT SAME TIME, when 44 (46, 48) sts rem, work 1 more WS row even, then beg neck shaping.

Neck shaping

Next row (RS) Mark center 14 (16, 18)

sts. Cont to work armhole decs as established, work to center marked sts, join 2nd ball of yarn, work center 14 (16, 18) sts, place them on a holder, then work to end as established. Working both sides at once and cont to work armhole shaping, bind off from each neck edge 3 sts once, 2 sts twice. Bind off rem 4 sts each side.

FRONT

Work as for back.

SLEEVES

With smaller needles, cast on 26 (26, 30) sts. Work in k2, p2 rib for 2"/5cm, dec 2 (0, 1) sts on last WS row—24 (26, 29) sts. Change to larger needles. Work in St st as foll: Work 2 rows even.

Next (inc) row (RS) K1, M1, work to last st, M1, k1. Rep inc row every 6th row 2 (2, 6) times more, then every 8th row 5 (5, 2) times—40 (42, 47) sts. Work even until piece measures 16½ (16¾, 16½)"/42 (42.5, 42)cm from beg, end with a WS row.

Raglan cap shaping

Work as for back armhole shaping. Bind off rem 4 (4, 5) sts.

FINISHING

Block pieces to measurements. Sew raglan sleeve cap to raglan armholes.

Collar

With RS facing and circular needle, pick up 64 (68, 72) sts evenly around neck. Join and work in rnds of k2, p2 rib for 2"/5cm. Bind off loosely in rib. Sew side and sleeve seams.

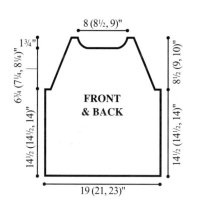

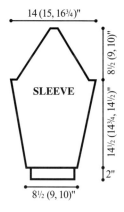

Two sizes of cables add a twist to this chic sleeveless pullover, featuring a face-framing cowl neck and tweedy hand-dyed yarn. Designed by Mari Lynn Patrick.

SIZES

Instructions are written for size Small. Changes for sizes Medium and Large are in parentheses.

KNITTED MEASUREMENTS

- Bust 33 (35, 37)"/84 (89, 94)cm
- Length 20½ (21, 21½)"/52 (53, 54.5)cm

MATERIALS

- 7 (7, 8) 3½oz/100g hanks (each approx 103yd/94m) of Colinette Yarns *Hand-dyed Zanziba* (wool/viscose/nylon⑤) in #76 lichen
- One pair each sizes 10 and 10½ (6mm and 6.5mm) needles *or size to obtain gauge*
- Sizes 10 and 10½ (6 and 6.5mm) circular needles, 16"/40cm long
- Cable needle

GAUGE

17 sts and 18 rows to 4"/10cm over pat sts using larger needles.
Take time to check gauge.

STITCH GLOSSARY

C3R

Sl 2 sts to cn and hold to *back*, k1, k2 from cn.

8-st RC

Sl 4 sts to cn and hold to *back*, k4, k4 from cn.

Note

Odd-numbered rows of chart are WS rows. Read these rows from left to right. Even-numbered rows of chart are RS rows. Read these rows from right to left.

BACK

With smaller needles, cast on 62 (66, 70) sts. **Row 1 (RS)** P2 (0, 2), [k2, p2] 1 (2, 2) times, [k3, p2] twice, [k2, p2] 8 times, k3, p2, k3, [p2, k2] 1 (2, 2) times, p2 (0, 2). Cont in rib as established for 1½"/4cm, end with a RS row. Change to larger needles.

Next row (WS) K6 (8, 10), [p3, k2] twice, *[p2, M1 purlwise] twice, p2, k2*; rep between *'s 3 times, p3, k2, p3, k6 (8, 10)—70 (74, 78) sts.

Beg chart

Row 2 (RS) P6 (8, 10), work sts 1 to 30, then sts 11 to 30 once, sts 1 to 8, p6 (8, 10). Cont to foll chart in this way through row 15, then rep rows 8–15 until piece measures 13"/33cm from beg.

Armhole shaping

Bind off 3 (3, 4) sts at beg of next 2 rows, 2 sts at beg of next 2 rows, dec 1 st each side every other row 0 (2, 3) times—60 sts. Cont in pat as established until armhole measures 6 (6½, 7)"/15 (16.5, 18)cm.

Neck and shoulder shaping

Bind off 2 sts from each shoulder edge 3 times, AT SAME TIME, bind off center 38 sts and working both sides at once, bind off 5 sts from each neck edge once.

FRONT

Work as for back until armhole measures 4 (4½, 5)"/10 (11.5, 12.5)cm.

Neck shaping

Next row (RS) Work 16 sts, join 2nd ball of yarn and bind off center 28 sts, work to end. Working both sides at once, bind off 2 sts from each neck edge 5 times. When same length as back, bind off 2 sts from each shoulder edge 3 times.

FINISHING

Pin pieces on a flat surface to measurements. Spray lightly with water and leave to dry. Do not block or press. Sew shoulder seams.

Cowl neck

With smaller circular needle, pick up and k 92 sts evenly around neck edge. Work in k2, p2 rib for 4"/10cm. Change to larger circular needle and cont in rib until cowl neck measures 11"/28cm. Bind off loosely in rib. Sew side seams.

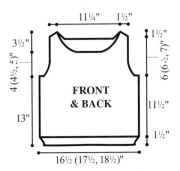

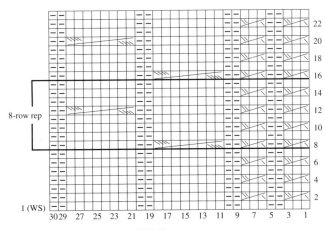

Stitch Key

☐ K on RS, p on WS

⊟ P on RS, k on WS

▧▧ C3R

▨▨▨ 8-st RC

Classic cabernet

Funky, fluffy yarn transforms a traditional Peruvian ch'ullu shape into a thoroughly modern must-have. Pom-poms trim seed-stitch ear flaps, and the stockinette crown decreases to an I-cord nub at the very top. Designed by Lipp Holmfeld.

KNITTED MEASUREMENTS

- Head circumference 19"/48cm
- Depth 7"/17.5cm

SIZE

One size fits most.

MATERIALS

- 2 1¾oz/50g balls (each approx 90yd/82m) of Berroco, Inc. *Furz* (nylon/wool/acrylic⑤) in #3838 red
- One set (4) size 10 (6mm) dpn *or size to obtain gauge*
- Size 10 (6mm) circular needle 18"/46cm long
- Size 8 (mm) crochet hook
- Stitch marker

GAUGE

14 sts and 24 rows to 4"/10cm over seed st using size 10 (6mm) needles.
Take time to check gauge.

SEED STITCH

Row 1 *K1, p1; rep from * to end.
Row 2 K the purl sts and p the knit sts.
Rep row 2 for seed st.

INC 1

K into front and back of st.

CAP

With crochet hook, ch 50 to make one tie. Sl st to one dpn and work first earflap on dpn as foll:
Row 1 Inc 1—2 sts.
Row 2 K1, inc 1—3 sts.
Row 3 K1, p1, inc 1—4 sts.
Row 4 P1, k1, p1 inc 1—5 sts.
Rows 5 and 6 Beg with a p1, work in seed st.
Row 7 *P1, k1; rep from * to last st, inc 1—6 sts.
Row 8 *K1, p1; rep from * to last st, inc 1—7 sts.
Rows 9 and 10 Beg with k1, work in seed st.
Row 11 *K1, p1; rep from * to last st, inc 1—8 sts.
Row 12 *P1, k1; rep from * to last st, inc 1—9 sts.
Rep rows 7–12 once—13 sts.
Rep rows 7–10 once—15 sts.
Cut yarn and leave sts on needle.
Make a second earflap in same way, but transfer this earflap to circular needle and cast on 24 sts for front of hat, work rem earflap onto needle, working in seed st, cast on 13 sts for back, pm.

Crown

Join and cont in seed st on 67 sts for 32 rnds (approx 4"/10cm). P 5 rnds, k 5 rnds, dec 1 st at end of last rnd—66 sts. Divide sts evenly over 3 dpn (22 sts on each needle).

Dec Rnd 1 *K9, k2tog; rep from * around—60 sts. K 1 rnd.
Dec Rnd 2 *K8, k2tog; rep from * around—54 sts. K 1 rnd.
Cont in this way to dec 6 sts every other rnd until 2 sts rem on each needle. Work 6 rnds even for tip. Cut yarn and pull through sts.

FINISHING

With tapestry needle and yarn, pass a running st around crown to form tuck. Make two 2"/5cm pom-poms and attach to end of ties.

Blending soft colors and softer cashmere, this elegant wrap by Fiona Ellis is a sensual delight. The alternating colors of the entrelac are repeated in a diagonal-stitch border and an edging of seed-stitched and pom-pom-topped triangles.

■ 19" x 72"/48cm x 183cm

■ 4 1¾ oz/50g balls (each approx 165yd/152m) of Trendsetter Yarns *Dali* (cashmere④) in #201 green (A)
■ 4 balls in #169 lilac (B)
■ One pair size 9 (5.5mm) needles *or size to obtain gauge*
■ Size 9 (5.5mm) circular needle, 16"/40cm long

■ 16 sts and 24 rows to 4"/10cm over St st using size 9 (5.5mm) needles.
■ 11 sts to 4"/10cm over entrelac pat using size 9 (5.5mm) needles.
Take time to check gauges.

Seed st
Row 1 (RS) *K1, p1; rep from * end, k1.
Row 2 K the purl sts and p the knit sts.
Rep row 2 for seed st.
Slip st pat
Row 1 (RS) With A, k3, sl 1, *k2, sl 1; rep

from * to last st, k1. **Row 2** P1, *sl 1, p2; rep from * to last st, p1. **Row 3** Change to B, k1, *sl 1, k2; rep from * to last st, k1. **Row 4** P3, sl 1, *p2, sl 1; rep from * to last st, p1. **Row 5** Change to A, k2, *sl 1, k2; rep from * to end. **Row 6** P2, *sl 1, p2; rep from * to end.
Rows 7 and 8 With B, rep rows 1 and 2.
Rows 9 and 10 With A, rep rows 3 and 4.
Rows 11 and 12 With B, rep rows 5 and 6.

With A, cast on 83 sts. Work 1 row in seed st. Change to B and work 2 rows garter st. **Next row (RS)** Change to A work 12 rows sl st pat. K 2 rows. **Next row (RS)** Change to B, k1, *k2tog; rep from * to end—42 sts.
Beg entrelac pat
Base triangles–*Next row (WS) With B, p2, turn; k2, turn; p3, turn; k3, turn; p4, turn; k4; cont in this way, working 1 more p st every other row until there are 6 p sts (1 triangle complete). Rep from * to end.
First row of rectangles
Beg edge triangle–Next row (RS) With A, k2, turn; k1, p1, turn; inc in first st, ssk, turn; k1, p1, turn; inc in first st, p1, put yarn in back, ssk, turn; [k1, p1] twice, k1, turn; inc in first st, p1, k1, p1, put yarn in back, ssk (edge triangle complete).
Rectangles
*Pick up and k6 sts evenly along edge of next triangle, turn; beg with k1, work 6 sts in seed st, turn; beg with p1, work 5 sts in seed st, ssk; rep last 2 steps 6 times (1 rectangle completed). Rep from * to * across row, to edge of last triangle.

Ending edge triangle

Pick up and k6 sts evenly along edge of this triangle, turn; p2tog, work 4 sts in seed st, turn; work 5 sts in seed st, turn; k2tog, work 3 sts in seed st, turn; work 4 sts in seed st, turn; p2tog, work 2 sts in seed st, turn; work 3 sts in seed st, turn; k2tog, p1, turn; k1, p1, turn; p2tog, leave rem st on RH needle, cut yarn.

Second row of rectangles

With B, cont from st on RH needle, pick up p 5 sts evenly along edge of triangle just worked. [Turn; k6, turn; p5, p2tog] 6 times. *Pick up and p6 sts evenly along side of next rectangle, [turn; k6, turn; p5, p2tog] 6 times; rep from * to end. Cut yarn.

Third row of rectangles

With A, work as for base triangles, but pick up sts along side edge of rectangles instead of triangles.

Cont to work in entrelac pat until work measures 64"/162.5cm from beg.

Final row of triangles

With B, cont from st on RH needle, pick up and p5 sts evenly along edge of triangle just worked, turn; k6, turn; p5, p2tog, turn; k5, turn; p4, p2tog, turn; k4, turn; p3, p2tog, turn; k3, turn; p2, p2tog, turn; k2, turn; p1, p2tog, turn; k1, turn; p2tog. Rep from * to end, picking up

sts from side of rectangles instead of triangles. Change to A, k1, inc 1 st in every st to end—83 sts. Change to A, k 1 row. Change to B, beg with row 3 of sl st pat and work rows 3-12, then rows 1 and 2. K 2 rows. Change to A, k 1 row. Bind off. Slip st borders (work along each long edge) With RS facing, using A and circular needle, pick up and k 368 sts. K 1 row. Change to B, beg with row 3 of Sl st pat and work rows 3-12, then rows 1 and 2. K 2 rows. Change to A, k 1 row. Bind off.

Border edge triangles

(Work along each short edge after sl st borders have been worked.) With RS facing, using A and circular needle, pick up and k 96 sts. K 1 row.

Next row K2, turn; k1, p1, turn (cont in seed st throughout); work 3, turn; work 3, turn; work 4, turn; work 4, turn; work 5, turn, work 5, turn; cont in this way until work 12 sts on both rows have been worked. Bind off 12*. With 1 st left on RH needle, change to B, k1. Rep from * to *. Work 6 more triangles along edge in this way, alternating colors for each triangle.

FINISHING

Make pom-poms. Sew in ends. Block. Sew on pom-poms.

RESOURCES

US RESOURCES

Write to the yarn companies listed below for purchasing and mail-order information.

BERROCO, INC.
PO Box 367
Uxbridge, MA 01569

BROWN SHEEP CO.
100662 County Road 16
Mitchell, NE 69357

CHERRY TREE HILL YARN
PO Box 659
Barton, VT 05822

CLASSIC ELITE YARNS
300 Jackson Street
Bldg. 5
Lowell, MA 01852

CLECKHEATON
distributed by
Plymouth Yarn

COLINETTE YARNS
distributed by
Unique Kolours

FILATURA DI CROSA
distributed by
Tahki•Stacy Charles, Inc.

GGH
distributed by
Muench Yarns

HORSTIA
distributed by
Muench Yarns

JCA
35 Scales Lane
Townsend, MA 01469

JUDI & CO.
18 Gallatin Drive
Dix Hills, NY 11746

K1C2, LLC
2220 Eastman Ave. #105
Ventura, CA 93003

KARABELLA YARNS
1201 Broadway
New York, NY 10001

LANE BORGOSESIA
PO Box 217
Colorado Springs, CO 80903

LION BRAND YARN CO.
34 West 15th Street
New York, NY 10011

MUENCH YARNS
285 Bel Marin Keys Blvd.
Unit J
Novato, CA 94949-5724

NATURALLY
distributed
S. R. Kertzer, Ltd.

PATONS®
PO Box 40
Listowel, ON N4W 3H3

PLYMOUTH YARN
PO Box 28
Bristol, PA 19007

REYNOLDS
distributed by
JCA

ROWAN YARNS
5 Northern Blvd.
Amherst, NH 03031

S. R. KERTZER, LTD.
105A Winges Road
Woodbridge, ON L4L 6C2
Canada

SCHULANA
distributed by
Skacel Collection, Inc.

SKACEL COLLECTION, INC.
PO Box 88110
Seattle, WA 98138-2110

TAHKI•STACY CHARLES, INC.
8000 Cooper Ave.
Glendale, NY 11385

TRENDSETTER YARNS
16742 Stagg Street
Suite 104
Van Nuys, CA 91406

UNIQUE KOLOURS
1428 Oak Lane
Downingtown, PA 19335

CANADIAN RESOURCES

Write to US resources for mail-order availability of yarns not listed.

BERROCO, INC.
distributed by
S. R. Kertzer, Ltd.

CLASSIC ELITE YARNS
distributed by
S. R. Kertzer, Ltd.

CLECKHEATON
distributed by
Diamond Yarn

DIAMOND YARN
9697 St. Laurent
Montreal, PQ H3L 2N1
and
155 Martin Ross, Unit #3
Toronto, ON M3J 2L9

ESTELLE DESIGNS & SALES, LTD.
Units 65/67
2220 Midland Ave.
Scarborough, ON M1P 3E6

FILATURA DI CROSA
distributed by
Diamond Yarn

NATURALLY
distributed by
S. R. Kertzer, Ltd.

PATONS®
PO Box 40
Listowel, ON N4W 3H3

ROWAN
distributed by
Diamond Yarn

S. R. KERTZER, LTD.
105A Winges Rd.
Woodbridge, ON L4L 6C2

SCHULANA
distributed by
Diamond Yarn

UK RESOURCES

Not all yarns used in this book are available in the UK. For yarns not available, make a comparable substitute or contact the US manufacturer for purchasing and mail-order information.

ROWAN YARNS
Green Lane Mill
Holmfirth
West Yorks HD7 1RW
Tel: 01484-681881

SILKSTONE
12 Market Place
Cockermouth
Cumbria, CA13 9NQ
Tel: 01900-821052

THOMAS RAMSDEN GROUP
Netherfield Road
Guiseley
West Yorks LS20 9PD
Tel: 01943-872264

Editor-in-Chief
TRISHA MALCOLM

Art Directors
CHRISTINE LIPERT
CHI LING MOY

Executive Editor
CARLA S. SCOTT

Managing Editor
SUZIE ELLIOTT

Contributing Editor
BETTY CHRISTIANSEN

Instructions Editors
KAREN GREENWALD
REBECCA ROSEN

Schematics
CHARLOTTE PARRY

Knitting Coordinator
JEAN GUIRGUIS

Yarn Coordinator
VERONICA MANNO

Editorial Coordinators
KATHLEEN KELLY
MICHELLE LO

Photography
BRIAN KRAUS, NYC
BOBB CONNORS
Photographed at Butterick Studios

Stylists
MONICA GAIGE-ROSENSWEIG
MELISSA MARTIN

Production Managers
LILLIAN ESPOSITO
WINNIE HINISH

■

President, SoHo Publishing Company
ART JOINNIDES